The Complete Caregiver Support Guide

A Reproducible Workbook for Groups and Individuals

by Ester R.A. Leutenberg & Carroll Morris
with Kathy Khalsa, OTR/L

Illustrated by Amy L. Brodsky, LISW-S

Duluth, Minnesota

Whole Person
101 West 2nd St., Suite 203
Duluth, MN 55802

800-247-6789

books@wholeperson.com
www.wholeperson.com

The Complete Caregiver Support Guide
A Reproducible Workbook for Groups and Individuals

Printed in the United States of America

10 9 8 7 6 5 4 3 2 1

Editorial Director: Carlene Sippola
Art Director: Joy Morgan Dey

Library of Congress Control Number: 2012936860
ISBN: 978-1-57025-265-5

We dedicate this book to our loved ones for whom we have been caregivers.

Special thanks to . . .

Kathy Khalsa, who guided us through the structure of our book and gave us the benefit and experience of her years as a psychiatric occupational therapist.

Amy Brodsky, whose artwork clearly captures the essence of the handouts in this book.

Esta Goldstein, who at an early morning breakfast, inspired this book as she lovingly related information about the *Saddlebrook Stroke and Neurological Caregiver Support Group*. She created it in her community when her husband had a stroke. She has continued with it long after he passed away.

Bebe Lewis, who shared her wisdom and care-giving experiences during the time her husband, Harold, was ill.

Thanks to the following who have reviewed this book and provided us with their insights.

Tani Bahti, RN, CT, CHPM

Howard Ball, PhD

Victoria L. Barnes

Joann M. Boyink

Carol Butler, MS Ed, RN, C

Payton Davies

Joanna Fitzgerald

Esta Goldstein, M.Ed.

Cynthia Holmes, PhD

Ora Keller

Sherokee Ilse

Jay L. Leutenberg

Patricia Mote, R.N.

Charlene Ostlund

Eileen Regen, M.Ed, CJE

Bonnie Scott

Linda Stein

Tyler Woods, PhD

Kathy A. Khalsa, OTR/L

Ester Leutenberg & Carroll Morris

The Complete Caregiver Support Guide
Table of Contents

Introduction

Chapter 1
Caregiver Support Groups

Chapter 2
Support Group Openers and Closers

Chapter 3

Self-Care for the Caregiver

Chapter 4

Communication

Chapter 5

Family and Close Friend Dynamics

Chapter 6

Being an Advocate for your Care-Receiver

Chapter 7

Record-Keeping

Chapter 8

Resources

Introduction
to the
The Complete Caregiver Support Guide

The Complete Caregiver Support Guide – A Reproducible Workbook for Groups and Individuals is a creative tool for professional facilitators and lay leaders seeking meaningful ways to make a difference in the lives of caregivers, care-receivers. It is also both a guide and comfort to the men and women caring for people of any age in need of significant support.

This introduction includes a brief history of caregiving and a discussion of what is involved in caregiving, the chapter contents and how to use the reproducible handouts.

The intention of this book is to provide educational content for support group facilitators and caregivers that touches on crucial topics. The reproducible handouts and worksheets provide insights, encourage problem-solving and develop the caregivers' ability to ask for the help they need to stay physically, mentally, emotionally and spiritually healthy, as they continue to be there for their care-receiver.

I always say that whenever a person gets sick, they need advocates.

It's very hard when you are dealing with the fear and the pain, and all the options and all the side effects. So you really need one or even two advocates. My husband had been very ill and I felt frequently that I had to be his advocate, challenging this doctor and that medicine. I felt it was really important because he was overcome and he was frightened. He had a brain aneurism. The person who is ill often can't think. He or she can't even figure out what's the next thing to do for themselves. So somebody has to be around, and I think that caregivers are the ones who can do that. They are probably the ones that will have to make the call.

~ Olympia Dukakis

About Caregivers

Former First Lady Rosalynn Carter stated,

"There are four kinds of people in this world: those who have been caregivers, those who currently are caregivers, those who will be caregivers, and those who will need caregivers."

This includes virtually everyone!

A Brief History of Caregiving

In past generations, it was customary for people to have large families. Members of an extended family often lived within a few miles of each other. Few women had jobs outside the home, so the elderly and infirm were cared for within the family. Both the primary caregiver and care-receiver had the support of nearby relatives, friends and community.

Circumstances are different today. Families are typically smaller and are often scattered across the country and around the globe. A much larger percentage of women work outside the home. People live longer, often with chronic illnesses. These factors make caregiving much more complicated than it was in the past.

The early stage of caregiving is often handled by family members or by friends who live near the person needing help. They begin by simply doing what they can and often, as time passes, assume the caregiver role without realizing it – caregiving isn't a job that many people choose to sign up for.

The tasks caregivers perform can vary widely, from transporting a child with disabilities to school each day, to doing someone else's laundry, to helping with medications, to dealing with insurance companies. Caregiving can be temporary, as when someone is recovering from an accident, or long-term, as when caring for a person in need of significant ongoing support.

(Continued on the next page)

About Caregivers *(Continued)*

In an attempt to define family caregiving, the National Family Caregivers Association (NFCA) developed a list called "Caregiving Is." The text below was inspired by that list.

Caregiving is as diverse as the individuals needing it. It can be 24-hour care for persons who cannot manage daily tasks of living or are suffering a significant level of cognitive loss. It can be preparing for an uncertain future because a spouse has a progressively disabling disease, even though that person is still able to function quite well. It can be temporary, last several years or last a lifetime.

Caregiving means being a person's healthcare advocate. It requires learning to work with doctors and other health care professionals and to navigate government healthcare programs. It can also be learning what it means to die with dignity and making sure that the care-receiver's wishes will be honored.

Caregiving is stressful work. Most people have had no training or education regarding the many aspects of caregiving when they begin helping their care-receiver. They discover that caregiving is assuming tasks they never dreamed of undertaking. It can be learning about medications, wheelchairs, lifts and gadgets that help struggling fingers button a shirt. It can involve doctor visits, calls to 911 and long days and nights in a hospital waiting or emergency room.

Caregiving challenges people to go beyond their comfort zone. It is having conversations on topics most people hope they will never need to address. It is grappling with questions that often have no easy answers. It is loving, giving and sharing. It is accepting, adapting and being willing to keep on going.

Caregiving forces individuals to deal with change. They are often required to re-evaluate finances, living conditions and/or their personal work situation. They will need to make compromises and readjust again and again as the circumstances change.

Caregiving is an endless search for balance. It is seeking the middle ground between doing too much for the care-receiver and doing too little. It is trying to find time for personal needs – and hopefully, even wants – while providing for another's needs. It is recognizing that one cannot do it alone – one can and should ask for help, respite care and time off for a vacation to recharge through activities that help maintain a sense of self.

Caregiving is a strain on relationships. Even the best of relationships can be challenged by the stress of caregiving. The demands on one's time and energy may leave family members or friends feeling neglected. Moving a parent into a family home – or moving into the parents' home – can be a source of contention between couples, and between parents and their children. Finances and other emotionally charged issues can also cause tension between adult children of an ailing parent.

(Continued on the next page)

About Caregivers *(Continued)*

Caregiving can be a lonely world. While the tasks and experiences of caregiving may be similar in nature, surprisingly they are not what unites family caregivers. According to the National Family Caregivers Association, the common bond of caregiving is the emotional impact.

Those caring for others often feel lonely, isolated, and unacknowledged for all their work and sacrifice. They can experience anger and resentment toward family members and others who carry on as usual, while they of necessity give up much of their normal life. They grieve the losses in their own lives as well as and the loss of the person their care-receiver once was as they watch him or her decline. They often experience depression, sadness, pain, the need for normalcy and regret for what they might have done had circumstances been different. They also may feel guilty because they sometimes wish it were over.

Caregivers can find comfort in learning that such feelings are perfectly normal and in finding ways to cope with them in support groups and within these pages. They can also find hope in the possibility of connecting on a deep level with their care-receiver and creating closer bonds with family members. In fact, discovering positive meaning in the tasks of caregiving is crucial for the emotional health of everyone involved.

Caregiving can also be moments of joy and fulfillment.

- Happiness when seeing one's child with a developmental disability learn a new skill.
- Joy when a spouse's face lights up, expressing thanks for being his or her partner on a difficult path.
- Closeness during nighttime conversations about love, life, death, and what's most important.
- Satisfaction in the knowledge that one has provided something for the care-receiver that has made life better.
- New recognition of one's inner strength and determination.
- Gratitude for simple things, for each new day.

Caregiver Stress: The Good, the Bad and the Ugly

Caregiving requires a great deal of emotional, physical, mental and spiritual energy. Given all that it entails, it is not a surprise that caregivers suffer from stress. The cost of that stress – whether short-term or chronic – on the caregiver's health can be significant.

The Good

Stress (or the stress response) is what you feel when your body prepares to meet a challenge. It goes into a fight-or-flight mode, releasing a flood of adrenaline and cortisol. The breath quickens, the heart beats faster and the senses sharpen. The body readies for action both when the danger is immediate and real and when it is a matter of perception.

When short term, the stress response is beneficial. It helps us react quickly to avoid accidents. It keeps us sharp. It provides the endurance to keep going beyond our normal strength. When the threat – perceived or real – passes, the stress level lessens and the body returns to normal. Long-term stress is another story.

The Bad

When a real or perceived threat to well-being or the need for action is ongoing, the stress response remains activated, releasing hormones over an extended period of time. The body acclimates to being in a defense mode. It turns on the stress response more quickly and leaves it on longer.

Many people in today's fast-paced, complicated world live with chronic stress. They may come to depend on the accompanying adrenalin lift and feel down in its absence. But chronic stress has health consequences. Studies indicate that the majority of doctor's visits are for stress-related complaints.

The list is long. Stress exacerbates health conditions such as asthma and arthritis. It weakens the immune system, making us vulnerable to illness. It can cause headaches, high blood pressure, chronic fatigue, digestive tract problems, higher incidences of diabetes, and sleep disorders. It can have a negative affect on memory and judgment, cause depression and anxiety, and lead to substance abuse.

The Ugly

If you're a caregiver, your situation can be a perfect storm of chronic stress.

(Continued on the next page)

Caregiver Stress: The Good, the Bad and the Ugly *(Continued)*

You might …

- be responsible for the physical, mental, and emotional care of your care-receiver, which means you always have to be on.
- have days full of tasks, some of them physically difficult and/or unpleasant.
  feel angry and frustrated – and then guilty – which increases your stress level even more.
- not be eating well, getting enough sleep or exercising.
- not be feeding yourself, mentally, emotionally and/or spiritually.
- be criticized for your actions.
- feel abandoned and alone; feel like there's no one to call on for help.
- be grieving daily losses as your care-receiver's condition worsens.
- be faced with questions regarding end of life issues.
- feel emotionally out of control or that there is little you can control.

Bottom line – If you're a caregiver, you're likely to be stressed, and caregiver stress can be detrimental to your health and well-being.

Various studies indicate that anywhere from 30 to 50 percent of caregivers over the age of 55 will die before the person for whom they are caring. Taking care of yourself is not self-indulgent – it is necessary!

As you travel through this workbook, you will discover many pages that invite you to assess your level of stress and help you to find ways to better take care of yourself. There's a reason for this. Caregivers tend to ignore their own needs. You, like others in your situation, may need to be often reminded of the importance of **your** health and welfare.

If **you** can no longer care for your loved one, who will?

If **you** become injured or ill, who will be your caregiver?

Don't Be Discouraged: Find Your Community – Find Your Voice

The task you have undertaken is challenging, and it is very important that you do not try to do it on your own.

Although family members and friends can offer help and support, they cannot understand what you're going through in the same way that another caregiver can. Belonging to a community of people dealing with the same issues will allow you to safely share your feelings in an atmosphere where you can all gain from each other's experience, ideas and wisdom.

It's also imperative that you find your voice – the strength and self-confidence to be an advocate not only for your care-receiver but also for yourself.

Where can you find your community and your voice?
In a caregiver's support group or an online caregiver's chat room.

About *The Complete Caregiver Support Guide*

Family members, and sometimes close friends, are often called upon to act as caregivers to ill or aging people they care about or for whom they are responsible. The time these courageous and dedicated caregivers spend with their care-receivers* can have many rewarding outcomes. However, caregivers are usually unprepared, untrained and unsupported. They are often isolated. These factors can put a huge amount of stress on non-professional or unprepared and unsupported family caregivers.

Attending a caregiver support group that focuses on specific issues is of great benefit for caregivers. Such groups are those facilitated by professionals such as social workers, counselors and group facilitators, as well as those facilitated by lay persons, often themselves caregivers.

Although this book is designed for use in support groups, individual caregivers seeking ways to manage the stresses of their role, will also find help within these pages. While most handouts and worksheets can stand alone, some sections that include explanatory information precedes them. It is not necessary that handouts and worksheets be used in any particular order. Depending on the needs of a particular group, facilitators can choose single sheets for discussion or delve into one of the longer sections over two or more meetings.

After completing the handouts, individuals can discuss their insights and questions with someone they can trust to give useful feedback, as well as family members who are willing to help in ways that will contribute to the caregiver's continued wellbeing.

*Rather than using a variety of phrases to describe the person who is a recipient of care, we have chosen to use the respectful word, *care-receiver* throughout the book.

(Continued on the next page)

About *The Complete Caregiver Support Guide*

(Continued)

Summary of Chapters' Content

Chapter 1. The Caregiver Support Group

Organizing and facilitating a support group can be a difficult job, even for professionals in the helping community. It can be even more daunting for lay persons.

This chapter covers …

- understanding the need for a support group
- organizing and advertising
- preparing for a meeting
- leading a meeting
- using activities effectively

Chapter 2. Support Group Openers and Closers

The pages in this chapter can be used either as a launching pad for a meeting or as a closing thought. For example, *The Caregiver's 7-Ups* and *How Am I Doing Right Now?* are especially effective when used as a participant check-in.

Chapter 3. Self-Care for the Caregiver

The challenge for caregivers involved is finding the balance between taking care of another and taking care of themselves. This chapter consists of single-sheet handouts that motivate participants to develop strategies that assist in maintaining the balance without which caregivers cannot be effective. It also has multiple page sections on important topics such as *My Emotional Wellbeing* and *Avoiding Caregiver Burnout*.

Chapter 4. Communication

Caregivers are called upon to communicate effectively in difficult or emotionally charged situations. Preparing for and having sensitive conversations with the care-receiver are helpful ways to improve communications. This chapter focuses on effective communication with suggestions on how to communicate when the care-receiver is confused or difficult to work with, as well as how to be more empathetic.

(Continued on the next page)

About *The Complete Caregiver Support Guide*

(Continued)

Summary of Chapters' Content *(Continued)*

Chapter 5. Family and/or Close Friends Dynamics

To be effective, caregiving must involve others beyond the primary caregiver, namely family members, whether nearby or far away, and/or other concerned individuals. This chapter includes a section giving the caregivers guidance on how to hold family meetings to discuss the care-receivers' current health, finances and end-of-life issues, plus how the caregivers can ask for what they need to avoid burnout. It also has ideas for handling the holidays and visits to the care-receiver.

Chapter 6. Caring for the Care-Receiver

In most cases, primary caregivers become the healthcare advocate for their care-receivers. This chapter focuses on what is necessary for effective advocacy, including doctor's visits, crisis preparation and home safety.

Chapter 7. Record Keeping

Caregivers can be so burdened with daily tasks that they can overlook the importance of keeping records. The reproducible forms in this chapter will help the caregiver with expenses tracking, healthcare-related conversations, medication administration and hospitalizations. The *Substitute Caregiver's Information* is invaluable for providing the data needed for another to take over in the caregiver's absence, whether for a few hours, a day or a longer period of time.

Chapter 8. Resources

Lists of suggested *Resource Books* related to caregiving, and *Disease-Related Websites* and *Other Pertinent Websites* are provided.

Using Chapter Reproducible Handouts

We encourage group facilitators to personally complete the handouts they intend to use for a given session. They may discover insights pertaining to their own lives, which will also help them in understanding the position of others. The issues facing caregivers are, in their essence, common to humankind in general - the need to communicate clearly, to be understood, to express emotions appropriately, to solve problems, and to create a support system. Refer to *Use of Reproducible Handouts*, page 17.

For the Facilitator
How to Use Reproducible Handouts

Why Use Reproducible Handouts

The use of handouts in group settings is extremely beneficial. They provide a beginning, middle and end to an activity to ensure completion of a topic. They offer the group leader a focus that can be useful when group members stray from the topic or continue with one point too long. They ensure an easy flow to the group session by directing members to follow the activity with text and visual cuing.

The reproducibility of handouts allows every participant to have their own copy, not only for the activity during the meeting itself but also to take home afterwards for further reflection and sharing. On pages where there aren't sufficient lines for the participants' responses, suggest they write or the reverse side.

Ways to Use Handouts in Groups

- Photocopy or print handouts for each group member. Involve them through volunteer or assigned reading.
- Distribute pens, pencils or highlighters to group members to encourage active participation by writing answers, comments or emphasizing certain points.
- Ask group members to share thoughts, ask questions or self-reflect as the session progresses.
- Invite group members to explain why the topic of the handout is relevant for caregivers.
- Summarize at the end of the session for a sense of closure.
- Use handouts as a take-home activity and review insights at the beginning of the next session.
- Provide group members with folders to store handouts.

Alternative Ways to Use Handouts

- Begin with a song, inspirational quote or poem related to the session theme.
- Use the graphics as conversation starters.
- Offer members the opportunity to lead a discussion. Provide volunteers with the handout one week before the session. This will ensure adequate preparation time.
- Bring personal examples for each handout. When discussing humor, be prepared with some favorite jokes. When discussing self-care, bring in your own self-care toolbox.
- Encourage caregivers to share and discuss appropriate handouts and insights with their care-receivers.

Using Quotations and Affirmations

The quotation and affirmation pages are designed to be copied, perhaps laminated, and cut into cards. As a session opener, cards can be passed out to participants or placed in a container participants can draw from. Give them a moment to ponder their quote or affirmation. Invite them to share their insights with the group. Copies of these handouts can also be given to support group participants to use at home.

Caregiver Support Groups

CHAPTER 1

ORGANIZING AND FACILITATING A SUPPORT GROUP can be a challenging job, even for professionals in the helping community. It can be even more so for lay persons. This chapter covers reasons for starting a group, organizing and advertising, preparing for and facilitating a meeting, and using activities effectively.

The Complete Caregiver Support Guide is filled with reproducible activities.
(Refer to *How to Use Reproducible Handouts*, page 17.)
It will provide you with many ways to lead successful support groups and bring creativity, personality and adventure to the meetings.

Keep meetings interesting . . .

Breathing exercises
Light exercise
Guided imagery
Outdoor meetings
Refreshment break
Silly video
Positive affirmations
Sing-along
Yoga
Walk, skip or tiptoe down the hall

Laughter yoga
March in place
Walk down the hall
Calm music
Jokes
Meaningful quotations
Potluck lunch
Warm cups of tea
Stretching
Finger paint with shaving cream

Why a Caregiver Support Group?

People who have been caring for a family member with a chronic or terminal illness know that it is a challenging job, one they cannot do alone. They need the companionship, understanding, and empathy of others on the same path.

Friends and family often step in to provide assistance and a listening ear, but unless they are immersed in the situation with the primary caregiver, they can't understand it the way another caregiver can. A support group can be very helpful – a safety net, in fact – for the caregiver.

A caregiver support group is:

A place that . . .

- provides confidentiality, thus allowing people to share freely
- offers the comfort of knowing others are experiencing similar issues
- helps caregivers to manage feelings of guilt and resentment
- reduces feelings of isolation
- offers a support network that may go beyond the group setting

A place to share . . .

- information
- coping strategies
- solutions to common problems
- techniques for dealing with family members

A place to learn . . .

- about the care-receiver's illness
- how to communicate with the care-receiver, family members and medical staff
- how to be a medical advocate for the care receiver
- how to manage caregiver stress
- the importance of taking care of yourself

Finding a Caregiver Support Group

To discover if there is an existing group in your area:

- Look online for *caregiver support groups* (search by your city or county). If the city or county health department sponsors a group or teaches classes for caregivers, it should appear in the search results.

- Also search using the name of your care-receiver's illness plus your location (*Alzheimer's* and your *county* or *city*). Services available in the area will appear in the search results.

- Check the websites of organizations that may have local programs or affiliated support groups.

  Family Caregiver Alliance – www.caregiver.org/caregiver/jsp/home.jsp

  National Alliance for Caregiving – www.caregiving.org/

  Caregiving.com – www.caregiving.com/

- Ask the local hospital's social services person if the hospital sponsors or can recommend a group.

- Ask your doctor, clinic or local hospice for information.

- Research local places of worship, libraries or community meeting places to see if they have an outreach program of benefit to caregivers.

If there isn't a support group specific to the care-receiver's situation or a general caregiver group in your area, consider starting one.

Organizing a caregiver support group is no small task. It will take time, energy, enthusiasm, organization and an ongoing commitment. It will also take other committed individuals willing to take on assignments to keep a group running smoothly. But the benefits are worth the effort.

Starting a Caregiver Support Group

STEP 1 – Contact other caregivers with the same need as yours.

Finding family caregivers interested in joining a support group may be easier than you think. According to the study *Caregiving in the U.S.* (2009), caregivers make up 29% of the adult population. Some of them may be looking for a support group right now. So start by getting the word out.

1. **Call, email or talk to:**
    - family, friends, neighbors, people in the doctor's office.
    - your care-receiver's doctors, nurses and social workers.
    - home health care providers and therapists.
    - religious and/ or spiritual leaders and teachers.
    - illness-specific organizations.
2. **Create a flyer** announcing an organizational meeting.
3. **Distribute flyers** to organizations and people who can assist you in spreading the word. Post the flyers where other caregivers will see them.
4. **Write an article** for your local newspaper or community newsletter.

STEP 2 - Meet with interested people to explore the possibility of a group.

1. **Call a meeting** of caregivers who have indicated interest in forming a group.
2. **Brainstorm**
    - Identify the needs and wants from a group of care-givers.
    - Create guidelines for the programs and the discussion.
    - Establish guidelines for ensuring confidentiality.

STEP 3 – Get down to the *nitty-gritty* of organizing your group.

Once you have elicited needed information, and you are confident there is enough interest to justify going forward, the real work of organizing begins. The next several pages cover points that are crucial to starting on the right foot. The worksheet, *Organizing a Caregiver Support Group*, page 27, will assist you in structuring your group.

Points to Consider When Starting a Support Group

There is a great deal to think about when organizing your group and this section will help you stay on track. Provide potential members with a copy and ask them to review it prior to the next meeting.

Working together, use the following information to guide you in filling out the worksheet, *Organizing a Caregiver Support Group*, page 27. Don't labor too much over it. Changes can be made later, if the group agrees it is necessary. The important thing is to complete it, so you will have a solid basis for moving forward.

1. **What kind of group are you organizing?** You are organizing a support group for anyone currently caring for a family member or friend.

2. **What will you call your group?** Brainstorm for ideas. You may wish to add something unique to the name, such as location, e.g., *Madera Caregiver's Support Group*.

3. **Who will be invited to attend?** Several configurations are possible. Caregivers only, caregivers and care-receivers together (not usually recommended, since it isn't always conducive to honest sharing), or caregivers and care-receivers meeting at the same time but in separate rooms.

   The benefit of the last option is that caregivers will not need to make arrangements for their care-receivers during this time. The downside is that arrangements would have to be made for someone to facilitate the care-receiver meetings.

4. **What is your purpose?** Using the information you have gathered through brainstorming, work together to create a mission statement. This will be the guiding principle of the group. It will help you decide how you want to proceed, what atmosphere you wish to create and assist in program planning.

   If you need help developing your mission statement, refer to the definitions of a caregiver on page 10. The example below from *The Parkinson's Caregiver's Support Group of Green Valley / Sahaurita* may also give you ideas.

Caregivers' Support Group Mission Statement

The mission of our group is to provide an encouraging and non-judgmental environment in which participants can freely share their experiences, concerns and solutions; learn new information and skills; and find friendship, empathetic listening, humor and examples of grace under pressure.

(Continued on the next page)

Points to Consider When Starting a Support Group

(Continued)

5. **What size will the group be?** Initially your group may be small, and that's okay. Generally groups of six to twelve allow for meaningful sharing and discussion. The key to success is keeping a meeting well organized and managed so that, regardless of the group's size, anyone wanting to share will be afforded the opportunity.

6. **Will you collect dues?** It is not necessary; however, doing so will give the group funds to use for speaker honorariums, sending cards to members, providing refreshments, etc. Another option is to request participants put what they can in a donation basket at each meeting.

7. **When and where will you meet?**

   When?

   Choose the day of the week and time that works for the majority of the interested caregivers.

   Will you meet once a month? Twice a month?

   Will you meet in the morning or afternoon? What time?

   How long will meetings last?

   Where? You probably want a space that has no fee attached, is available long-term at your chosen time, and has adequate handicapped or close-in parking. To assist you in narrowing your search, review the pros and cons of the following options:

   - A participant's home – This may be convenient but it can put stress on the person who is hosting. Rotating homes can be confusing, however it can work if people volunteer and keep it simple for all involved. Keep in mind, whatever you choose, liability and privacy issues could surface.
   - Community room in a condo or apartment complex – These facilities work well. Check if parking and kitchen privileges are available, if needed.
   - Public Library and Senior or Community Centers – These often have available rooms, wheelchair accessibility and a message or announcement board where a flier advertising the group can be posted. But be aware that some people may feel uncomfortable meeting in a public place.
   - Places of worship – These are excellent for privacy. However, some people may be uncomfortable if they aren't affiliated with the particular institution.
   - Hospitals or Medical Centers – If they have rooms available, potential guest speakers may be close-by. Some hospitals may charge for parking and some people may not want to come into a clinical setting.

(Continued on the next page)

Points to Consider When Starting a Support Group

(Continued)

8. **Who will lead your group?**
   Some support groups are lead by professionals such as a mental health therapist, social worker, or someone in the field of gerontology or health care. Such professionals are often willing to donate their time and experience, especially if they have been a caregiver. Other groups are led by one member, or by members taking turns at facilitating. The advantage of having lay leaders is they can speak from, and empathize through, personal experiences.

   Even if no one in your group has professional qualifications, you may find members with other qualifications that would make them good leaders.

   Look for someone who . . .
   - has had experience teaching or leading groups or meetings
   - feels comfortable in a leadership position
   - displays warmth and empathy
   - is reliable

   If your volunteer leader hasn't had experience facilitating a group, refer to the suggestions for planning and leading meetings, *Guidelines for Group Leaders*, page 30 and *How to Lead a Meeting*, page 31.

9. **What other leadership roles are necessary for your group to run smoothly?**
   If your group is small, you may not feel a need for a formal roster of officers. A designated support group facilitator with others volunteering to do certain tasks, such as room setup, will suffice. As your group expands, you may choose to formalize your structure. If so, spend part of one meeting discussing the needs of the group, what might be helpful and how members might contribute, to keep the group running smoothly.
   Below are some of the leadership roles (besides the facilitator/group leader) to consider:

   Treasurer – collects dues or donations

   Program Chair – lines up speakers

   Membership Manager – keeps member contact list current

   Communications – handles e-mail or phone reminders of upcoming meetings and sends information from the meetings to those not in attendance. This person may also write articles for newspapers, newsletters, etc

   Sunshine Chair – sends cards to members, or makes phone contact with those who need a pick-me-up

   Facility Manager – sets up the room prior to each meeting and is the liaison to the contact person of the meeting facility

(Continued on the next page)

Points to Consider When Starting a Support Group

(Continued)

10. **How will you structure your meetings?**
 It is a challenge to balance the need to promote information and solutions with the need to share personal experiences and receive support and encouragement.

 Which of the following fits your group's needs?

 - **Sharing and Open Discussion:** In this type of meeting, participants can unburden themselves and receive feedback, empathy and support. They are also encouraged to share insights and solutions. If desired, the meetings can have an educational component, with assigned members presenting a short spotlight on a topic following the sharing time.
 - **Education:** In this more formal meeting, an outside speaker addresses topics of interest followed by discussion and/or activities.
 - **Combination:** This type of group will alternate meetings with outside presenters and meetings focused on sharing and discussion.

11. **What will your ground rules be?**
 Members of a support group come with the assumption they will be able to share personal information safely. For this to happen, there needs to be an agreement among members as to how they will listen and respond to each other. It is also important to have an understanding of the confidentiality policy. These outcomes can be achieved by setting ground rules at the beginning.

 Examples of Support Group Ground Rules
 - We begin and end our meetings on time.
 - We will respect and maintain the confidentiality of the group.
 Personal information is not to be repeated or discussed at any other time or place.
 - We do not discuss group members who are not present.
 - We each share the responsibility for making this group work.
 - We avoid making judgments. We accept people for what they bring to the group.
 - We have the right to speak and we have the right to remain silent.
 - We have the right to ask questions and the right to decline to answer.
 - We will give everyone an opportunity to speak.
 - We will share our own feelings, experiences and gentle advice.
 - We try to be aware of our own feelings and talk about what is present in our lives now.
 - We will speak from our own experiences instead of generalizing
 Start our comments with I instead of they, we and you).
 - We will listen actively and give supportive attention to the person who is speaking.
 - We will avoid side conversations.
 - We will avoid interrupting. If we do break in, we will return to the other person's conversation.
 - We will be conscious of body language and nonverbal responses – they can be as disrespectful as ill-chosen words.

Organizing a Caregiver Support Group

1. **Name**____

2. **Mission Statement**
   The purpose of *(Group's Name)* ____________________________

   is to ____

3. **What is the projected size of your group?**____________________

4. **When and where will you meet?**________________________

5. **Who will lead your group?** __________________________

6. **What other officers/helpers will you have?**____________________

7. **How will you structure your meetings?**
   Indicate desired balance between education, sharing personal knowledge and sharing current emotional and physical state.

8. **What are your ideas about ground rules?**

Getting the Word Out!

Create a flyer advertising your first meeting.

Distribute flyers to the people and locations mentioned in Step One, page 22.

State clearly the time and place of the meeting.

(example: The Sun City Oro Valley Parkinson's Support Group will meet the third Wednesday of every month at 10 a.m. at the library on the corner of First and Main.)

When you have a special speaker, make a flyer specifically for that meeting. Speakers often draw a larger-than-usual crowd. On occasion, consider inviting the general public.

Write an article about caregiving or send a press release to the local newspaper.

Mention or email information to everyone you know. People who are not caregivers may know and contact others who are.

Submit information to:

- community event calendars
- local newspapers
- radio
- cable networks
- spiritual and religious institutions' newsletters

Post flyers in: *(ask for permission)*

- libraries
- grocery stores
- clinic waiting rooms
- senior citizen buildings
- places of worship
- doctors' offices where people who deal with the same issue will frequent.
- community centers
- social services offices of hospitals and clinics

Once Your Group is Up and Running ...

Before the meeting:

1. **Reserve your space** a year in advance, if possible.
2. **Ask a member to be responsible** for set-up.

   Arrange chairs in a circle or around tables

   Set up sign-in table

      Sign-in sheet – use to create a membership list

      Stick-on "Hello" tags or plastic name holders

      Handouts

      Water, glasses and tissues

3. **Arrange your program** a month or more in advance, especially if you are having speakers.

   Give speakers a clear description of your group and what members want them to address. Make sure they have your contact information and directions to the meeting place. Check with them a week before the meeting to find out if they need a flip board, digital projector for a Power Point presentation or any other materials. Many professionals in mental and physical health care enjoy speaking and often will not charge a fee.

   Some speaker suggestions to get you started:

   - Doctors, nurses, and occupational, physical, or speech therapists
   - Social workers, counselors, experts in stress management
   - Assisted living, skilled nursing, hospice liaisons
   - Yoga, QiGong, Tai Chi, other exercise instructors
   - Hypnotist, chiropractor, audiologist, herbalist, massage or aroma therapist, reflexologist
   - Non-denominational minister, spiritual counselor
   - Humorist, storyteller

   If possible, give presenters an honorarium or other 'thank-you' gift, even if they offer their services for free. This is one reason to consider having dues or a donation basket at each meeting.

4. **Create, maintain and use a contact list.**

   You can build your contact list by having first-time attendees fill out a card with their name, address, phone number, and e-mail address. Have them indicate if they are willing to share this information with others in the group for networking purposes. Update the list as necessary after each meeting. Use it to inform members of upcoming programs and for other necessary communications.

5. **Encourage networking** – Pass out the contact information of those who have agreed to share it, so members who wish to do so can talk on the phone or get together between meetings.

Guidelines for Group Leaders

1. Arrive early to greet participants by name. Smile.

2. Acknowledge each person's sharing. Reflect what you have heard them express, taking into account non-verbal communication. Ask if others have something to contribute.

3. Help participants tread the fine line between expressing empathy and getting caught up in the intense emotions of the person who is sharing. Also, help them toe the line between offering suggestions (in the form of their own experiences) and trying to solve the person's problems.

4. Offer suggestions from experience rather than giving advice. The group is for support, not therapy.

5. Remind everyone that thoughts and feelings are not right or wrong. Encourage non-judgmental responses.

6. Notice who is participating in discussions and who isn't. Attempt to elicit responses from those who are not speaking, but honor their wish if they prefer not to speak.

7. Allow only one person to speak at a time. Consider a "talking stick," flower or teddy bear to pass. The one holding the item is the only one who can speak.

8. Keep discussions at a personal level. Encourage "I" statements. Remind participants that the meeting is about and for caregivers, not about the condition of the care-receiver, except when discussing current circumstances of the caregiver.

9. Notice the group dynamic. Are people interested and engaged in what's being said? Are some looking down as if bored? Is the topic causing some to be uncomfortable because it's too negative or sad or is going on too long? Acknowledge the speaker's communication, and then gently lead the group on to something new.

10. Redirect the conversation if one person is taking too much time. The group is for everyone.

11. Be prepared to handle emotional distress. Many caregivers bottle their feelings until they blow up or are in a place where it's safe to express themselves. A support group offers that safe place. Even so, the group leader will need to handle such situations carefully. Have tissues nearby.

    - Thank him or her for trusting the group with the situation.
      Be sure he or she feels acknowledged, supported and valued.
    - Avoid probing into a sensitive personal situation.
    - Ask if others have been in the similar situations and invite them to share their solutions.
      This shifts conversation from emotion-sharing to information-sharing.

How to Lead the Meeting

1. **Start** on time.

2. **Welcome** new members. Invite them to share their reasons for coming to the group. At all times, respect anyone's desire to not share.

3. **Conduct** any group business; make announcements.

4. **Describe** the group's mission and guidelines.
   This can be done by reading the mission statement at the beginning of each meeting. It acts as an orientation for newcomers as well as a reminder for returning members.

5. **Read** the group's confidentiality policy.

6. **Participant check-in.**
   This is a brief statement of how caregivers are doing, not a report on everything that's happening with their care-receiver, although they are intertwined.

   Use questions on *How Am I Doing Right Now*, page 36.
   Ask "starter" questions, such as "What is working well in your job as caregiver?"
   or "Did anything significant change for you since the last meeting?"
   These questions may elicit lengthy responses. It's important to continue to move around the circle, but also let participants know you'll return to them if they have more they need to talk about.

7. **Main body of meeting.** Use one or more of the ideas below, being aware of time.

   a. Educational segment with outside speakers or a member reporting on assigned topic or topic of choice, followed by discussion.

   b. Use one of the worksheets in this book as focus for the meeting with discussion and work time.

   c. Split into smaller groups for in-depth discussion of what's currently happening in caregivers' lives, plus sharing of solutions.

8. **Closing – always close on time!**

   Thank the speaker for the presentation. Thank participants for coming and sharing.
   Announce the topic/speaker for next meeting.
   End on a positive note.

   See Chapter 2, ***Support Group Openers & Closers***, beginning on page 33.

Support Group Openers & Closers

CHAPTER 2

THE PAGES IN THIS CHAPTER are to be used as a launching point for a support group or as a closing thought. They can be read by the facilitator, volunteers or each person reading a line or two, going around the room.

Want Ad for a Caregiver

WANTED:

Mother Theresa clone willing to relocate. Must be able to hear angry words without taking them personally; to be with other people's problems without getting weighed down; and to deal with unpleasant realities with patience, skill and humor. A plus if willing to cook, clean, manage finances, drive and get by on catnaps. Understanding of pain, grief and loss is a must. Salary will not be commensurate with duties performed; however, blessings will accumulate in heavenly savings account. Benefits include meaningful employment, knowing you made a difference, and gratitude and love from the family and care-receiver. Vacations are possible only when you can replace yourself.

~ Carroll Morris

Caregiver's Bill of Rights

Post this Bill of Rights in your bedroom and read it each morning.

I have the right to be told and relay the truth to the immediate family.

I have the right to be upset when I receive bad news about my care-receiver.

I have the right to talk about my care-receiver's illness when appropriate, or not.

I have the right to give constructive feedback, in a calm assertive way to a medical professional or establishment that is caring for my care-receiver.

I have the right to disagree with my care-receiver, even though he or she is ill.

I have the right to not accept on any attempt by my care-receiver (either conscious or unconscious) to manipulate me through guilt, anger or depression.

I have the right to engage outside help even though my care-receiver would prefer only me.

I have the right to look after my own needs as well as my care-receiver's needs. This is not an act of selfishness. It will increase my ability to care for him or her.

I have the right to enjoy my good health and do what it takes to keep it that way.

I have the right to recognize the limits of my own endurance and strength.

I have the right to get help for myself if I need to.

I have the right to receive consideration, affection, forgiveness, and acceptance from my care-receiver, when he or she is capable, providing I offer the same qualities.

I have the right to be free of verbal, emotional or physical abuse from my care-receiver or my care-receiver's family.

I have the right to feel what I feel, when I feel it.

I have the right to cry.

I have the right to be angry and depressed and to express difficult feelings occasionally.

I have the right to feel frustrated and/or angry and without feelings of guilt.

I have the right to seek humor in difficult situations.

I have the right to do some things just for myself.

I have the right to protect my individuality and make a life for myself that will sustain me for the time when my care-receiver no longer needs my full-time help.

I have the right to long for normalcy.

Care-Receiver's Bill of Rights

Read this with your care-receiver and then post it in your care-receiver's bedroom or main living area.

I have the right to be told the truth about my condition.

I have the right to be told if anything changes with my condition.

I have the right to ask questions of my health-care professional.

I have the right have an opinion about my health care.

I have the right to talk to anyone about my condition.

I have the right to be treated as a person who can make my own decisions.

I have the right to decide when and whom to ask for help in making decisions.

I have the right to give feedback to the medical community in an assertive way.

I have the right to give feedback to my caregivers in an forthright, but loving way.

I have the right to be treated with courtesy and respect, and to give that back in return.

I have the right to ask for help with the things I cannot do.

I have the right to be free of pain, if that is my choice.

I have the right to be free of verbal or physical abuse.

I have the right to respectful treatment of my property.

I have the right to assertively speak my mind and share my feelings.

I have the right to be angry at people I love and work it out with them in a respectful way.

I have the right to cry.

I have the right to be frustrated.

I have the right to feel bad if I receive bad news.

I have the right to not allow my illness/disease to control every moment of my life.

I have the right to think about other things besides my illness/disease.

I have the right to be hopeful.

I have the right to long for normalcy.

I have the right to wish for a miracle.

This handout can be discussed in a caregiver's meeting to evaluate how each member is respecting these rights.

How Am I Doing Right Now?

For the Caregiver and the Care-Receiver

What am I thinking right now? ____

____

What am I feeling right now? ____

____

On a scale of 1-10, how much stress am I feeling? (1 being the least) ______________________

____

What am I doing to help myself? ____

____

What more can I do to help myself? ____

____

What do I need the most right now? ____

____

Whom can I call on for support? ____

____

Ask yourself these questions periodically to stay aware of your current needs.

Caregivers may also wish to complete this handout periodically with their care-receiver.

You might want your care-receiver to respond to these questions, also.
Discuss your answers.

My Affirmations

I love myself.	I am aware of my own needs.
I am open.	I can ask for support and help.
I am kind to myself.	I eat healthy foods.
I exercise regularly.	I nurture myself.
I am compassionate with myself.	I am compassionate with others.

Cut out these affirmations and post them in a place where you will see them.

My Affirmations

I forgive myself.	I forgive my care-receiver.
I find time for fun.	I am at peace with myself.
I know I am doing the best I can.	I am whole and alive.
I AM ENOUGH.	**I am loved.**
I trust myself to do the right thing.	I trust my support system.

Cut out these affirmations and post them in a place where you will see them.

My Affirmations

Even when all else seems lost, I will give and accept love.	*I make time to take care of myself.*
I SEEK HELP AND ACCEPT IT WITH GRATITUDE.	Now matter how overwhelmed I am, I find at least one positive to focus on.
I draw strength from positive experiences from our past.	*I work with my care-receiver to make meaning out of our situation.*
I allow myself to feel my emotions.	I express my emotions appropriately.
WRITE YOUR OWN AFFIRMATION	WRITE YOUR OWN AFFIRMATION

Cut out these affirmations and post them in a place where you will see them.

The Caregiver's 7-Ups

1	Wake Up		Decide to have a good day.
2	Dress Up		Put on a smile and something colorful.
3	Shut Up	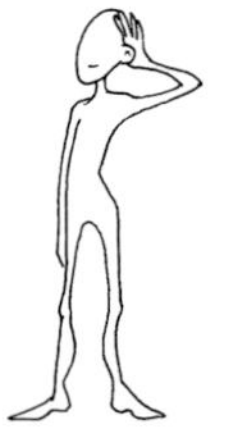	And listen to others and your inner self.
4	Stand Up		For yourself and your care-partner.
5	Look Up	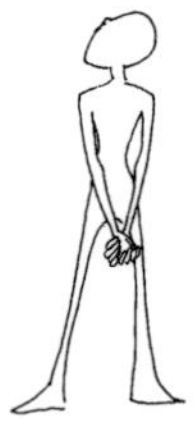	To whatever gives you strength.
6	Reach Up		Exercise will help release stress.
7	Lift Up		Your thoughts. Focus on something positive.

Wise Words to Ponder

The wise words below can help you keep your situation in perspective.

Cut these out and post them where you will see them.

Life isn't fair, but it's still good.	***It's OK to let your family see you cry.***	When in doubt, just take the small step.
Life is too short to waste time hating anyone.	You don't have to win every argument. Agree to disagree.	Make peace with your past so it won't mess up your future.
Don't compare yourself to others. You have no idea what their journey is all about.	Cry with someone. It's more healing than crying alone.	Take a deep breath. It calms the mind.
Over prepare then go with the flow.	However good or bad a situation is, it will change.	What do you want on your tombstone . . . ***I was right*** or ***I was loved?***

Helpful Idea Exchange

What did you do recently that was helpful to you as a caregiver?

Examples:

- *Found a tray that fits over the arms of my care-receiver's favorite chair.*
- *Put fluorescent tape along the floor from the bedroom to the bathroom.*
- *Hung a bell on the bedroom or bathroom doorknob.*
  During the night when my care-receiver gets up to go to the bathroom, the bell rings.
- *Picked up all the throw rugs.*
- *Put a baby monitor in my care-receiver's bedroom.*
- *Meditated 10 minutes first thing in the morning.*
- ______________________________
- ______________________________
- ______________________________
- ______________________________
- ______________________________
- ______________________________
- ______________________________
- ______________________________
- ______________________________
- ______________________________
- ______________________________
- ______________________________
- ______________________________
- ______________________________
- ______________________________
- ______________________________

Ask a group member to compile everyone's suggestions, photocopy and distribute them at the next meeting, or e-mail the list to the members.

Emotions Word Search

A	P	R	O	U	D	G	R	A	T	E	F	U	L	C	Z	D
F	0	U	C	D	A	G	F	E	A	R	I	R	T	H	E	S
U	Y	H	L	U	G	A	M	S	N	J	D	E	K	I	N	F
L	D	P	O	T	R	S	N	E	X	S	T	S	E	R	J	A
F	E	D	S	P	I	W	E	G	I	U	T	E	N	B	C	O
I	P	E	E	R	E	O	G	K	E	A	T	N	H	C	O	V
L	R	N	N	L	F	R	U	S	T	R	A	T	I	O	N	E
L	E	I	E	N	N	R	E	A	Y	M	Y	M	S	M	F	R
M	S	A	S	P	H	Y	I	B	A	R	G	E	I	P	I	W
E	S	L	S	K	I	L	L	S	L	L	U	N	E	A	D	H
N	I	M	A	T	N	I	G	R	S	T	I	T	O	S	E	E
T	O	T	S	Y	L	E	H	E	L	P	L	E	S	S	N	L
U	N	L	T	T	Y	L	E	L	R	E	T	V	A	I	T	M
M	C	A	R	I	N	G	O	I	S	E	L	L	L	O	V	E
E	A	V	E	I	D	A	R	E	W	A	R	D	I	N	G	D
R	I	D	S	A	T	I	S	F	A	C	T	I	O	N	Y	A
S	L	A	S	N	A	C	C	E	P	T	A	N	C	E	P	Z

Comfortable Emotions

ACCEPTANCE
CARING
CLOSENESS
COMPASSION
CONFIDENT
FULFILLMENT
GRATEFUL
HOPE
LOVE
PROUD
RELIEF
REWARDING
SATISFACTION

Uncomfortable Emotions

ANGER
ANXIETY
DENIAL
DEPRESSION
FEAR
FRUSTRATION
GRIEF
GUILT
HELPLESS
OVERWHELMED
RESENTMENT
STRESS
WORRY

As you are completing this word search, mark the emotions you most often feel, on the list above. What does this tell you? How can you lessen your uncomfortable emotions and connect more with the comfortable emotions?

Emotions Word Search – Solution

A	P	R	O	U	D	G	R	A	T	E	F	U	L	C	Z	D
F	0	U	C	D	A	G	F	E	A	R	I	R	T	H	E	S
U	Y	H	L	U	G	A	M	S	N	J	D	E	K	I	N	F
L	D	P	O	T	R	S	N	E	X	S	T	S	E	R	J	A
F	E	D	S	P	I	W	E	G	I	U	T	E	N	B	C	O
I	P	E	E	R	E	O	G	K	E	A	T	N	H	C	O	V
L	R	N	N	L	F	R	U	S	T	R	A	T	I	O	N	E
L	E	I	E	N	N	R	E	A	Y	M	Y	M	S	M	F	R
M	S	A	S	P	H	Y	I	B	A	R	G	E	I	P	I	W
E	S	L	S	K	I	L	L	S	L	L	U	N	E	A	D	H
N	I	M	A	T	N	I	G	R	S	T	I	T	O	S	E	E
T	O	T	S	Y	L	E	H	E	L	P	L	E	S	S	N	L
U	N	L	T	T	Y	L	E	L	R	E	T	V	A	I	T	M
M	C	A	R	I	N	G	O	I	S	E	L	L	L	O	V	E
E	A	V	E	I	D	A	R	E	W	A	R	D	I	N	G	D
R	I	D	S	A	T	I	S	F	A	C	T	I	O	N	Y	A
S	L	A	S	N	A	C	C	E	P	T	A	N	C	E	P	Z

Uplifting Quotations

Cut out these affirmations and post them in a place where you will see them.

I always try to balance the light with the heavy; a few tears of spirit, in with the sequins and the fringes.

~ Bette Midler

If you're going through hell, keep going.

~ Winston Churchill

Pain nourishes courage. You can't be brave if you've only had wonderful things happen to you.

~ Mary Tyler Moore

Laughter has always brought me out of unhappy situations. Even in your darkest moment, you usually find something to laugh about if you try hard enough.

~Red Skelton

The pessimist sees difficulty in every opportunity. The optimist sees the opportunity in every difficulty.

~ Winston Churchill

Once you choose hope, anything's possible.

~ Christopher Reeve

The sun shines all day long, even when there are clouds. What a great role model.

~ Sally Huss

Hope is the feeling we have, that the feeling we have is not permanent.

~ Mignon McLaughlin

It is not denial. I'm just selective about the reality I accept.

~ Bill Watterson

You will find peace not by trying to escape your problems, but by confronting them courageously. You will find peace not in denial, but in victory.

~ J. Donald Walters

Uplifting Quotations

Cut out these affirmations and post them in a place where you will see them.

A wise man adapts himself to circumstances as water shapes itself to the vessel that contains it.

~ Chinese proverb

Beginners and outsiders are open to possibilities and don't make assumptions. By extension, they're often better at finding solutions the experts have stopped seeing.

~ Michael McMillan

Humankind has not woven the web of life. We are but one thread within it. Whatever we do to the web, we do to ourselves. All things are bound together. All things connect.

~ Chief Seattle

You can learn new things at any time in your life if you're willing to be a beginner. If you actually learn to like being a beginner, the whole world opens up to you.

~ Barbara Sher

The best way to find yourself, is to lose yourself in the service of others.

~ Ghandi

When I let go of what I am, I become what I might be.

~ LaoTzu

It is one of most beautiful compensations of life, that no man can sincerely try to help another without helping himself.

~ Ralph Waldo Emerson

Become aware that there are no accidents in our intelligent universe. Realize that everything that shows up in your life has something to teach you. Appreciate everyone and everything in your life.

~ Wayne Dyer

... He'd done all he could. But choosing to lovingly care for her was like steering a plane into a mountain as gently as possible. The crash is imminent it's how you spend your time on the way down that counts ...

~ Jamie Ford

I've learned that every day you should reach out and touch someone. People love a warm hug, or just a friendly pat on the back.

~ Maya Angelou

Uplifting Quotations

Cut out these affirmations and post them in a place where you will see them.

Courage is not the absence of fear, but rather the judgment that something else is more important than fear.

~ Ambrose Redmoon

Everything has its wonders, even darkness and silence, and I learn, whatever state I may be in, therein to be content.

~ Helen Keller

It's easy to make a buck. It's a lot tougher to make a difference.

~ Tom Brokaw

Perseverance is not a long race; it is many short races one after another.

~ Walter Elliott

We start out as caregivers, but with time, we grow into care managers.

~ Gail Sheehy

Your title is "Fearless Caregiver Advocate." You want to gain the skills to become CEO of your family's "Caregiving, Inc."

~ Gary Berg

All successful caregivers need to know three things:

- *When to find help*
- *How to arrange breaks*
- *How to cope with runaway emotions*

~ Donna Schempp

Less stimulation, less activity, less conversation, and less pleasure in life lead to more and more depression, until the person has a declining ability to have any pleasure in any activity.

~ Dr. Hymayun

One step at a time is good walking.

~ Chinese proverb

The best and most beautiful things in the world cannot be seen or even touched. They must be felt with the heart.

~ Helen Keller

Uplifting Quotations

Cut out these affirmations and post them in a place where you will see them.

I've learned that you shouldn't go through life with a catcher's mitt on both hands; you need to be able to throw some things back.

~ Maya Angelou

One person caring about another represents life's greatest value.

~ Jim Rohn

When the world says "Give up," Hope whispers, "Try it one more time."

~ Author unknown

You give but little when you give of your possessions. It is when you give of yourself that you truly give.

~ Kahlil Gibran

Kindness is in our power, even when fondness is not.

~ Samuel Johnson

The art of being wise is the art of knowing what to overlook.

~ William James

Acceptance of what has happened is the first step to overcoming the consequences of any misfortune.

~ William James

Have patience with all things, but chiefly have patience with yourself.

~ Saint Francis de Sales

You have not lived today until you have done something for someone who can never repay you.

~ John Bunyon

I've learned that people will forget what you said, people will forget what you did, but people will never forget how you made them feel.

~ Maya Angelou

Self-Care for the Caregiver

CHAPTER 3

A MAJOR CHALLENGE FOR CAREGIVERS is finding the time to take care of themselves while caring for others. Doing so is crucial. If caregivers do not maintain their emotional and physical health, they may not be able to continue helping their care-receiver. This chapter consists of single-sheet handouts prompting participants to develop strategies for maintaining their own health and wellbeing.

Life Lessons We Can Learn From a Dog

We caregivers often live in the world of "what if?" We concern ourselves about and prepare for what the future might bring. We're always on guard. We focus on what we need to do rather than what we want to do. We get too serious. The following list suggests some delightful ways to lighten up, be present, and find joy in life's simple pleasures - as taught by man's best friend. Just reading it will make you smile. And you even might identify a line or two that can help you be as relaxed, warm and loving as a pooch!

Be loyal.

Take naps.

Stretch before rising.

Run, romp, and play daily.

Delight in the simple joy of a long walk.

Avoid biting when a simple growl will do.

Never pretend to be something you're not.

Thrive on attention and let people touch you.

If what you want lies buried, dig until you find it.

Never pass up the opportunity to go for a joyride.

On warm days, stop to lie on your back on the grass.

When loved ones come home, always run to greet them.

On hot days, drink lots of water and lie under a shady tree.

When you're happy, dance around and wag your entire body.

When someone is having a bad day, be silent, sit close by and nuzzle gently.

Allow the experience of fresh air and the wind in your face to be pure ecstasy.

Making Life Easier – Survival Strategies for the Stressed

It may sound simplistic, but it's true: Taking time to plan your day and organize your environment can go a long way toward reducing stress and helping you feel you have some control over your situation. With your lists in hand, you will not have to wonder what it is that you need to do, whom you plan to call, where you want to go or what you intend to buy.

If you do not accomplish everything you hoped to in a given day, move undone items to the next day, putting those of highest priority first. If you repeatedly move the same item forward, ask yourself: Why do I resist doing it? Is it important or necessary? Can someone else do it for me?

Strategies for minimizing daily stress and irritations:

1. Organize your environment *(cupboards, closets, a place for your keys, etc.)*
2. Go through mail daily *(sort, toss or keep)*
3. Make lists in a portable notebook/calendar you can keep with you *(to do, phone calls, groceries)*
4. Schedule a realistic day *(important things first, doesn't have to be perfect)*
5. Create a "What If?" plan *(what if my care-receiver wanders off when we're shopping?)*
6. Prepare the night before *(prepare meds, set table, review to-do lists)*
7. Rise before your care-receiver wakes *(read, shower, meditate, or enjoy a cup of tea or coffee)*
8. Do one thing at a time *(multi-tasking isn't always effective when you're stressed)*
9. Know your limits and learn to say No! *(protect your time, energy, health)*
10. Be prepared *(food and postage in the house, full gas tank, extra house and car keys)*
11. Keep up with maintenance *(fix, replace, maintain – yourself or ask someone)*
12. Take care of your own health *(have a physical exam, eat healthy, sleep well, exercise)*
13. Maintain good relationships *(apologize if needed, forgive others and yourself.)*

What will I do to make life less stressful? *(compare your responses with others in the room)*

1. ______________________________
2. ______________________________
3. ______________________________
4. ______________________________
5. ______________________________
6. ______________________________
7. ______________________________
8. ______________________________
9. ______________________________
10. ______________________________
11. ______________________________
12. ______________________________
13. ______________________________

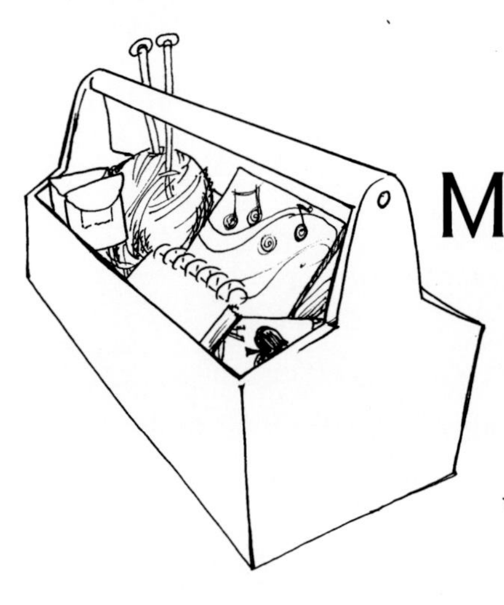

My Portable Self-Care Toolbox

Fill your Self-Care Toolbox with items sure to provide you with a pick-me-up in a free moment. Choose a container that you can carry easily (a portable file box, a large tote-bag or a small wheelie suitcase). Check the items you would like to have handy.

- ❑ A journal
- ❑ Box of tissues
- ❑ Calming tea
- ❑ Cell phone or iPad with an extra battery or charging cord
- ❑ Deck of cards
- ❑ Energizing healthy snacks
- ❑ Energizing, uplifting or relaxing music
- ❑ Enriching quotations
- ❑ Essential oils or flower essences to calm or energize
- ❑ Gratitude notebook
- ❑ Humorous books or DVDs
- ❑ Inspirational books
- ❑ "It Could be Worse" journaling book
- ❑ Knitting or any portable craft or hobby
- ❑ Meaningful affirmation cards
- ❑ Meditation, guided imagery or self-hypnosis CDs with portable music player
- ❑ Names, telephone numbers and e-mails of people you might want to contact
- ❑ Notebook , note cards or stationary and envelopes
- ❑ Notes or cards from someone expressing love and gratitude for you
- ❑ Pencils and/or pens
- ❑ Photographs of family (grandchildren, etc.)
- ❑ Pictures of inspirational people.
- ❑ Sketch pad and pencils
- ❑ Spiritual and/or religious reminders
- ❑ Sudoku or crossword puzzle books

Other ideas:

____

____

____

____

Adjusting to a New Normal ... Again!

Becoming a caregiver, especially to someone living with you, changes everything: your priorities, routine, demands on your time and the way your household is set up.

After what may be a difficult time of adjustment, life settles into a new routine. You've figured out what you need to do for your care-receiver and when. You've made changes so the living space is safe and comfortable. You're juggling - more or less successfully – your caregiving duties and other obligations. Life as it now is has become your new normal.

Then one day, you'll realize that your care-receiver's condition has noticeably changed for the worse. Tasks he/she could do may now be difficult or impossible. A visit to the doctor may result in changes to treatment or medication. The once comfortable routine no longer works. Again, you have to figure out what needs to change, implement doctor's suggestions, and adjust to the new circumstances ... to another new normal.

You may go through this recognition and adjustment pattern several times during your caregiving. Whenever your care-receiver's circumstances change in any way, complete the section below to help you gain insight and a new perspective.

Recently, what has changed in your care-receiver's situation? ________________________________

____

What does he/she need help with now? ________________________________

____

How has this affected your routine? ________________________________

____

What do you need to do differently? ________________________________

____

How can you help him/her adjust to these losses? ________________________________

____

Not only does progressive debility affect how and what needs to be done, it changes how care-partners relate to one another, particularly if they are spouses. The questions below may help you discover ways to remain close to your care-receiver.

What activity did you do together that is now too difficult? ________________________________

____

Can you continue to do it, but in a modified way? ________________________________

____

If not, what activity can replace it? ________________________________

____

Is there a way you connected emotionally that is no longer as effective? ________________________________

____

In what new way might you keep that connection alive? ________________________________

____

My Emotional Well-Being

Caregivers are often hard on themselves.
Their expectations are, to be able to:

- keep their own household going as usual
- keep their life as 'normal' as usual
- handle the finances
- address every physical, spiritual, intellectual and emotional need of the care recipient
- be a case manager or health advocate
- maintain a pleasant demeanor at all times.

That is an impossible task! So it's not surprising that caregivers feel as if they're not doing enough or that they've done something wrong. They are upset with themselves for not being patient or loving enough. They also feel guilty for wanting some time to themselves.

Keeping emotional balance is very important. Here are some ways you can shift your mood toward the positive.

Positive Self-Talk – We all have the voices in our head that make a running commentary on everything we do. Too often they're telling us how 'stupid' and impatient we are and what we could do better. Shift your focus whenever you realize that inner voice is beating you up. The more often you do, the less power you give those negative thoughts. Turn the negative self-talk in your head to positive self-talk.

What do I often tell myself that I'd like to change? (*Example: I should have been more patient.)*

What would I rather hear? *(I did the best I could and I will try to be more patient.)*

Forgive Yourself and Let Go of Your Guilt – People feel guilt because they think that somehow there's something they could, might, should do better. Know that you are trying to do the best that you can. Acknowledge what you've done that you wish you hadn't and create a strategy to avoid the same pitfall, and then let it go.

Love Yourself as You Are – Caregivers are special people and you are doing a huge job.

Say this to yourself, filling in the appropriate words.

"Even though I ______________________________________, I still love and accept myself."

Share Your Feelings – Sharing feelings with a special friend whom you can trust will keep them from building up.

Find a Way to Get a Good Laugh – Watch a funny movie or television show, etc.

Read a Book – Choose a book that is uplifting, and will distract and/or inspire you.

Address your Spiritual and/or Religious Needs – Talk with a religious or spiritual leader, attend a place of worship, read an inspirational book, pray, meditate, take a walk in a park, etc.

(Continued on the next page)

My Emotional Well-Being *(Continued)*

Acknowledge Everything You Do – Make a list of the many things you do that make a positive difference in your care-receiver's life – even the smallest things.

Discovering What Is Causing Your Anger and Frustration

1. What has happened that adds to your stress? ____________________

____

____

2. Has your care-receiver's circumstance changed for the worse? How? ____________________

____

____

3. What actions must you do for your care-receiver that you intensely dislike? ____________________

____

____

4. Do you feel overwhelmed? What do you wish family members or friends would do to help?____________________

____

____

5. What issues do you and family members or good friends disagree on, concerning your care-receiver's care?

____

____

6. What are you fearful of in the near future? ____________________

____

____

7. Are you feeling under-appreciated? Explain why. ____________________

____

____

8. Are you running out of energy or are you not feeling well? Explain.____________________

____

____

Look at your responses above. What is your most pressing need? What will you do about it?

The Guilts

All caregivers, at one time or another, will question how well they are caring for the person who is dependent upon them. You probably will, too, and then you may feel as if you have fallen short of your own and possibly others' expectations. You may feel what is known as caregiver's guilt.

When that happens, be gentle with yourself. You are human, doing the best you can in a difficult situation.

Here are some typical reasons caregivers feel guilty. Check those that apply to you and add your own.

- ❑ You are impatient at times.
- ❑ You speak abruptly or with a raised voice at times.
- ❑ You've had thoughts such as, "I wish this were over."
- ❑ You feel guilty about taking time for yourself.
- ❑ Your caregiving takes time away from your normal life and other people important to you.
- ❑ You've made decisions that you are now second-guessing.
- ❑ You can't make your care-receiver better, despite your best efforts.
- ❑ ______________________________
- ❑ ______________________________
- ❑ ______________________________
- ❑ ______________________________
- ❑ ______________________________

Unresolved feelings of guilt can hamper your ability to be a loving and effective caregiver. Once you have acknowledged the issues you feel guilty about, do not dwell on them. Let them go! Then decide what you can do better or differently.

Taking one or more of the steps below can help you maintain a balanced, healthy perspective.

- Remind yourself that what you do makes a difference.
- Set realistic goals.
- Accept your shortcomings and take action in areas you can improve.
- Do not take yourself too seriously.
- Arrange for a regular respite care, so you have time for yourself.
- Attend a support group as often as possible.
- Share your thoughts with a trusted friend or family member.
- Seek a therapist or counselor if you feel depressed over a prolonged period of time.

Give Yourself a Do-Over

No matter how hard you try to stay centered, calm, patient and loving, the combination of being tired, stressed, sleep-deprived and frustrated will eventually get to you. You may say things you promised yourself you would never say. You may do things you promised yourself, maybe that very morning, you would never do. Your care-receiver will get the brunt of it, but others might be affected, too. Family members, the checkout person in the grocery store, the person in line who is counting change when you're in a hurry, or a neighbor who inadvertently pushes your button.

When the frustration lifts, you will probably regret your loss of control. You will feel badly for having been rude, especially to your care-receiver, and for not being able to handle everything on your plate with more grace. You could carry the guilt on your back for months, even years after your caregiving is over. But you don't need to. Instead, call for a do-over – the chance to re-do an action with the possibility of doing better.

STEPS TO A DO-OVER

1. When you realize that you have crossed a line, **STOP** whatever you are doing or saying.
   Stop raising your voice; stop being sarcastic; stop blaming. If you can't do that, just stop talking.
2. **APOLOGIZE** immediately.
3. **RE-DO** the moment. Back up, start over, and say what you wish you had said.
4. **LET GO OF GUILT**. Nobody benefits by your carrying around a load of guilt, least of all you. Use this phrase: "*Even though I ______________________________, I still love and accept myself.*"
5. **DON'T SAY** *I'll never do that again.* You probably will, because you're human. However, you can cut down on the frequency and the intensity of your verbal blow-ups by having strategies in mind for coping with your anger and frustration.

WAYS TO LET OFF STEAM HARMLESSLY

1. Venting in appropriate ways can help you stay calmer and more in control. Here are some examples of ways to do that:
   - Let it all out in your journal.
   - Call a friend who is willing to be your sounding board and keep what you say confidential. There's a caveat, however. Dwelling endlessly on the situation will intensify your negative feelings. Give yourself a limited amount of time to vent. Be sure your friend understands that is all the time you get.
   - Take a quick brisk walk around the block to release some endorphins.
   - Take a few deep breaths and try to identify what caused the blow-up.
2. If your feelings are intense and persistent, it is important to identify the cause. Assess your situation. Decide what you need. Practice ways to manage the problem. Don't forget to call on friends and family for help. If your situation does not improve, you may need professional help.

For more insights complete the worksheet,
***Discovering What Is Causing Your Anger and Frustration*, page 55.**

Counting My Blessings

> ***When I started counting my blessings, my whole life turned around.***
>
> **~ Willie Nelson**

Caregivers and care-receivers often focus on the negatives and overlook the positives … the sunlight, the people we love and those who love us, and so much more. Take some time each day to think about your blessings and write them on this list. If you can easily come up with five, stretch the list to even more. Dig deep.

Sunday ____

____

Monday ____

____

Tuesday ____

____

Wednesday ____

____

Thursday ____

____

Friday ____

____

Saturday ____

____

In this variation of counting your blessings, challenge yourself to find something positive – perhaps even humorous – in an event you might otherwise view as negative.

Examples:

I am thankful that my eyelids are so heavy. It gives me a reason to stop and rest.

The flat tire was upsetting, but it gave me a chance to sit quietly while I waited for a tow.

The toast burned, but the oatmeal I had instead was so warm and comforting.

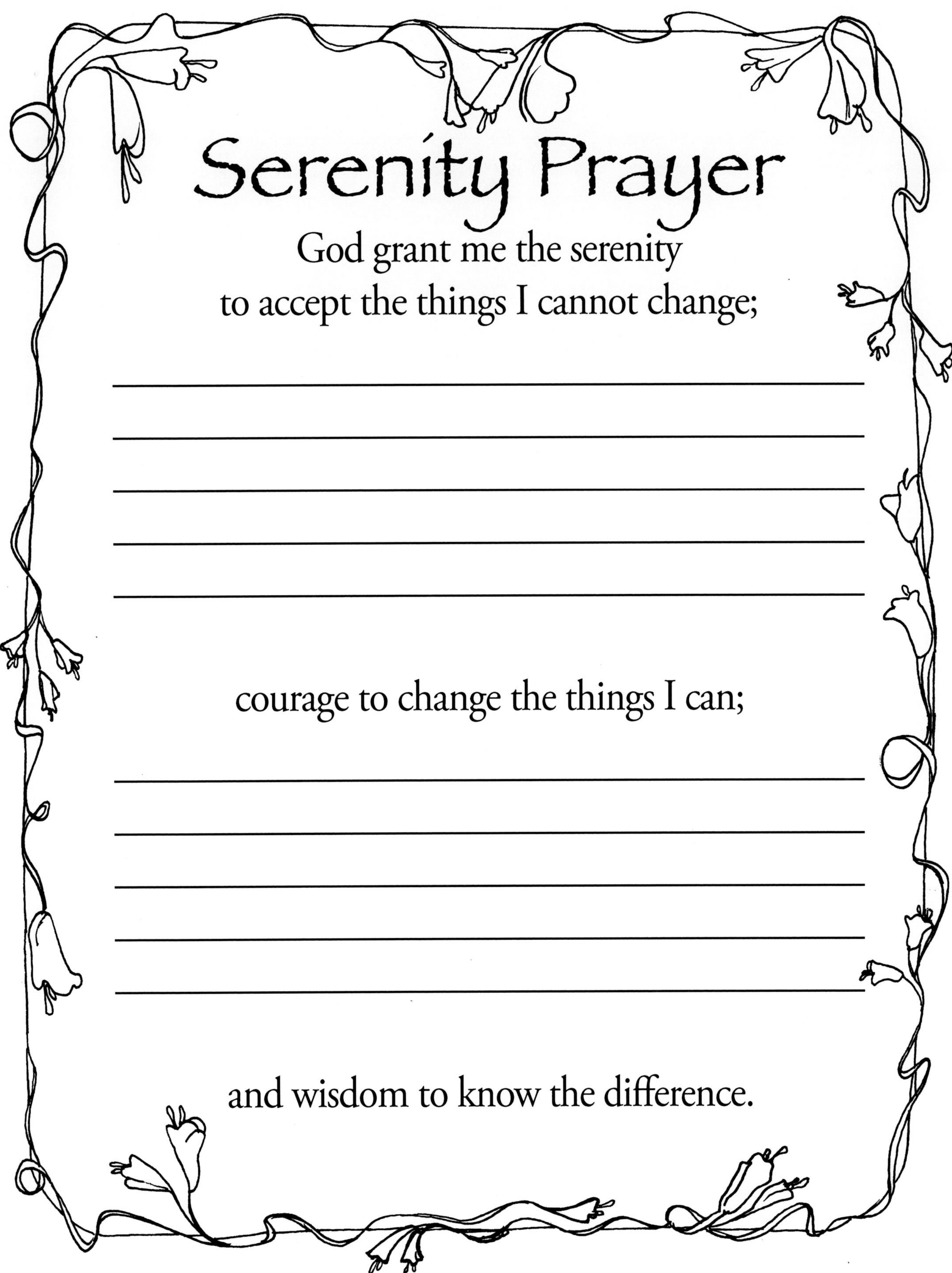

Serenity Prayer

God grant me the serenity
to accept the things I cannot change;

courage to change the things I can;

and wisdom to know the difference.

Personalized Serenity Prayer

God grant me the serenity

to accept

____
NAME OF CARE-RECEIVER

just the way ________ is;
HE / SHE

the choices ________ makes;
HE / SHE

the courage to change my reactions

to ________ and the circumstances;
HIM / HER

and the wisdom to let go of the things

I can't do anything about.

My TAKING CARE OF ME Monthly Schedule (✓ off daily)

MONTH ______________________

DAY	MEDS A.M.	MEDS NOON	MEDS P.M.	MEDS BEDTIME	OTHER MEDICAL	EXERCISE	CONNECT w/FAMILY	CONNECT w/FRIENDS	HAVE FUN	RELAX	FIND TIME FOR MYSELF	GET OUT OF THE HOUSE	EAT/DRINK HEALTHY	DRINK WATER	HUG CARE-RECEIVER
1															
2															
3															
4															
5															
6															
7															
8															
9															
10															
11															
12															
13															
14															
15															
16															
17															
18															
19															
20															
21															
22															
23															
24															
25															
26															
27															
28															
29															
30															
31															

END OF MONTH:

The patterns I have noticed ____.

I think I will do ____ differently.

A Guided Imagery Meditation

Guided imagery is a gentle but powerful technique for releasing tension and managing stress. It helps you use your imagination to lead you to a quiet, relaxed and peaceful state, where you are ready to repeat the affirmations on the following page. In a support group, your facilitator will read the guided imagery. At home, you can ask a friend or relative to read it, pausing wherever there are three periods. Or you can record it yourself for playback later.

Before you begin, find a quiet place, get comfortable and close your eyes. Breathe slowly and deeply. Listen.

Caregiver Stress
Belleruth Naparstek © 2008

Imagining a place… where you feel safe and peaceful and easy… a place you used to go to… or somewhere you've always wanted to be… and it doesn't matter if it's by the ocean… or in the woods… or up in the mountains or in the desert… just so it's a place that feels good and safe and peaceful to you… and allowing yourself to pick one place for now… knowing you can always change it next time…

And allowing the place to become real to you… in all its dimensions… looking around you… enjoying the colors… the scenery… looking over to your left… and over to your right…

And feeling whatever you're sitting against or lying upon… whether you're leaning against a friendly, wide oak tree… or surrounded by sweet meadow grass… or walking in the woods, on a fragrant carpet of pine needles.. or you might be at the beach, with cool, wet sand oozing between your toes, and gentle waves lapping at your ankles… or maybe you're just sitting on a nice, warm rock in the sun… it doesn't matter…

And you know that any place that feels safe and peaceful and easy… is exactly the right place for you to be…

And listening to the sounds of the place… letting your ears become attuned to all the beautiful sounds of this place… that is so safe and peaceful to you…

And smelling its rich fragrance… sometimes the air is so laden with scent, you can practically taste it on your tongue…

And noticing the feel of the air on your skin as it caresses your face and neck… and it might be crisp and dry… or balmy and wet… so you're just letting your skin enjoy the wonderful presence of this place… that is so safe and peaceful to you… and letting its healing presence soak into your skin… letting it fill you… permeating muscle and tissue and bone… all the way down into each and every cell…

So with every breath, you're inhaling the nourishing beauty of this place… breathing it into your heart… letting it soak into every corner of your being… infusing you with peace and calm…

Feeling the healing presence of this place… surrounding you with a cushion of gentle, healing energy… softly vibrating around you… and tingling on your skin… becoming more and more palpable… and you might be watching its sparkling dots of dancing color… feeling its caress as it lightly touches your skin… or hearing its gentle, humming song…

And inside, at the center of this force field, you can feel safe and protected… knowing you're able to take in whatever is nourishing to you… but insulated from whatever you don't want or need.

Affirmations to Minimize Caregiver Stress

Find a comfortable, quiet place. Take several deep breaths, exhale any tension and allow yourself to relax deeply. Read an affirmation. Say it aloud several times. Then close your eyes and let the meaning sink deep. You may not think the words are true for you, but let them work within you. Over time, they can have a powerful, healing effect.

More and more, I can let go of worrying about things I cannot control, and focus on my own inner peacefulness.

More and more, I am learning to be gentle and compassionate toward myself.

More and more I can respect my own natural limits and take the time I need to care for myself.

More and more, I am discovering that I am more capable and resourceful than I ever knew.

I treasure the moments of sweet connection that my love and care have brought me.

More and more, I can find ways to love and respect people in spite of the diminished circumstances they find themselves in.

More and more, I can take moments for self-care, and do what I need to do to replenish my body, mind and spirit.

More and more, I learn to love in new ways, even as I miss loving in the old ways.

More and more, I am learning to save my energy for what truly matters.

More and more I'm able to savor the gifts of the present.

More and more, I can take pleasure in the simple joys of living.

More and more, I understand that I cannot make this situation go away, but I can make it easier.

I can feel the love and care of friends and loved ones all around me, supporting my courage and lifting my spirits.

I am grateful for my own resilient courage and tenacity. I salute the fortitude I have shown and will continue to show.

I know I have things to do, purposes to accomplish, gifts to give, and that these things will come in their own good time.

~ by Belleruth Naperstek, MSW, Health Journeys

Helping Myself with Healthy Habits

A caregiver version of a well-known quote, *Eat, drink, and be merry,* might be *Eat, sleep and be merry.* If you only could! You prepare meals for your care-receiver but often eat on the run. You might only have memories of what a good night's sleep feels like, and the chances are you experience many days when you don't felt merry. However, good nutrition, getting as much good sleep as possible (yes, naps count), and learning to laugh despite your situation are all ways of fighting stress.

The handout below and the two following will give you ideas about healthy changes. Remember, even small changes can make a difference.

Simple Steps to Healthy Eating

Choose nutrient-rich foods: (whole grains, colorful fruits and vegetables, low-fat protein)

My Plan ______________________________

____

____

Eat breakfast: (provides needed fuel for your mind and body)

My Plan

____

____

Drink mostly water or herbal tea: (avoid caffeinated drinks and alcohol)

My Plan ______________________________

____

____

Keep healthy snacks handy: (reach for them when you need a snack)

My Plan ______________________________

____

____

Simplify cooking: (crock pot, omelets, sandwiches, soup)

My Plan ______________________________

____

____

(Continued on the next page)

Helping Myself with Healthy Habits *(Continued)*

Ways to Sleep More Restfully

Poor sleep can cause caregivers to be irritable and accident-prone. It can hamper the ability to think clearly and make good decisions. It affects physical health as well, since the body repairs and rejuvenates itself during a normal sleep cycle. Below are suggestions to help you get more and better sleep.

WHAT YOU CAN DO TO HELP YOUR CARE-RECEIVER:

Place a check ✔ by the items that you are willing to try and add your own ideas:

- ❑ Cut back on his or her caffeine, especially toward the end of the day.
- ❑ Prevent or reduce daytime napping, especially toward the end of the day, if possible.
- ❑ Encourage him or her to do the level of exercise of which he or she is capable.
- ❑ Avoid stimulating activities or television programs before bedtime.
- ❑ Create a calming bedtime routine.
- ❑ If possible, remove electronics and books from the bedroom.
- ❑ Assure that he or she is not hungry before bed.
- ❑ See the doctor to rule out a physical problem if care-receiver wakes you to go to the bathroom multiple times a night.
- ❑ Put a commode next to the bed, if necessary.
- ❑ Place nightlights in bedroom and hallways.
- ❑ Administer meds with water at least two hours before bedtime (unless to be taken with food).
- ❑ Other ____.

WHAT YOU CAN DO TO HELP YOURSELF

Place a check ✔ by the items that you are willing to try and add your own ideas:

- ❑ Walk a mile a day or engage in some other form of exercise.
- ❑ Take a 20-minute power nap, if possible (longer might make you groggy).
- ❑ Cut back on caffeine 4-6 hours before bedtime.
- ❑ Avoid stimulating activities or television programs.
- ❑ Establish a nighttime routine.
- ❑ Make a tomorrow's to-do list before bedtime, to avoid thinking about it when you are trying to sleep.
- ❑ Calm yourself with meditation, breathing exercises or a self-hypnosis CD.
- ❑ Have a cup of herbal tea.
- ❑ Rise early and take care of yourself first (meditate, plan the day, eat breakfast, exercise).
- ❑ Other ____.

FOR BOTH THE CARE-RECEIVER AND CAREGIVER

Make the environment best for sleep, a comfortable atmosphere: (pillow the right thickness, not-too-heavy coverings, mattress comfortable, just-right room temperature.) If you are still not sleeping enough, ask a relative or friend to sit with your care-receiver for a half-hour during the day so you can nap without worry. Perhaps you have someone who can stay overnight 2 or 3 nights a week so you can sleep undisturbed. If it is financially possible, have a home health aid care for your loved one during one or more nights a week.

(Continued on the next page)

Helping Myself with Healthy Habits *(Continued)*

Lighten Up!

Laughter reduces stress, aids digestion, helps people live longer, assists with creative problem solving and adds sparkle to one's life. It is contagious – laugh and others will laugh with you, including your care-receiver. Life will be easier for both of you if you can find the humor in your situation.

Here are some ways to lighten up. Rate yourself.

Do You . . .	**LOW**				**HIGH**
Smile often	1	2	3	4	5
Laugh at jokes	1	2	3	4	5
Say funny things	1	2	3	4	5
See the humor in a tense situation	1	2	3	4	5
Own a funny 365 day calendar	1	2	3	4	5
Play games and/or do puzzles	1	2	3	4	5
Watch humorous TV shows	1	2	3	4	5
Rent a funny movie	1	2	3	4	5
Be friends with people who have a good sense of humor	1	2	3	4	5
Laugh out loud at a movie	1	2	3	4	5
Watch comedians on television	1	2	3	4	5
Laugh with your care-receiver	1	2	3	4	5
Tell your care-receiver jokes or funny stories	1	2	3	4	5
Laugh at yourself	1	2	3	4	5
Read humorous comics or books	1	2	3	4	5

TOTAL ____________________

There is a possible score of 75. How do you think you rate?
Read these over again and put a checkmark by those you will regularly incorporate in your daily life.

**If you can't laugh, practice smiling.
It relieves stress, boosts your immune system, lowers blood pressure and releases feel-good neurotransmitters. And it makes you look younger!
That combination is hard to beat.**

Facing Reality

No one will see these answers but you!

Facing the truth and taking appropriate steps will give you the power and strength to keep going.

1. What are you feeling right now? ______________________________

____

2. On a scale of 1 (not very) to 10 (very), how stressed are you right now? Explain. ______________________________

____

3. What are you doing to help yourself cope?______________________________

____

4. What more can do you do to help yourself cope?______________________________

____

5. What help do you need most?______________________________

____

6. How can you get more help?______________________________

____

7. To whom can you talk when you need to vent? ______________________________

____

8. To whom can you talk, but haven't reached out to yet?______________________________

____

9. On a scale of 1 (not very) to 10 (very), how close are you to a meltdown? Explain.______________________________

____

10. If you rated yourself over 6, perhaps it's time to see your physician, a counselor or therapist. With whom can you make an appointment? ______________________________

____

11. If you do not know of anyone, to whom can you turn for a referral? ______________________________

____

12. What is one way you can find someone to give you more help with your care-receiver? ______________________________

____

Signs of Caregiver Burnout

When caregivers focus primarily on the needs of their care-receivers, they may neglect their own health and welfare. This places them at risk for stress-related illnesses, anxiety and depression. Thus, caregiver burnout. Recognized early, burnout can be avoided or treated, allowing caregivers to continue in their important role.

Do you have signs of caregiver burnout?
Check those that apply to you and then add to the list and consider discussing them.

❑ I wake up feeling exhausted, wondering how I'll get through another day.
❑ I blow up at the littlest thing, cry for no reason, or laugh when it's inappropriate.
❑ I drink a lot of caffeine to make it through the day and use alcohol to wind down at night.
❑ I don't spend much time with friends. I'm not interested in activities the way I used to be.
❑ I haven't had a decent night's sleep for some time.
❑ I feel hopeless. I wonder when it will be over. Then I feel guilty.
❑ I've gained or lost weight. I reach for snacks instead of eating a meal.
❑ I don't care or bother with how I look or what I wear.
❑ I often have headaches, colds or aches and pain.
❑ I'm oversensitive to comments people make about how I'm caring for my loved one.
❑ I don't remember what it's like to be happy.
❑ I sometimes neglect my care-receiver or treat him or her unkindly or roughly.
❑ I forget appointments and lose things. I can't concentrate.
❑ ____
❑ ____

Several checked boxes can be an indication that you need to arrange for regular respite care. This temporary care for the care-receiver will allow you run errands, exercise, keep your own doctor's appointments, meet with friends, etc. Relatives and/or trusted family friends are often willing to sit with a care-receiver for a few hours at a time. Consider employing a professional healthcare provider. If necessary, ask family members to contribute to the cost.

What steps are you willing to take? Check those that appeal to you and list other ideas below.

❑ Ask family members or good friends to take over specific tasks or provide respite care.
❑ Keep a calendar showing who is going to help and when.
❑ Participate in activities important to your health and well-being:
meditate, exercise, visit friends, resume a hobby.
❑ Fill your shelves with items you can make into quick, nutritious meals. (See *Simple Steps to Healthy Eating*, page 64.)
❑ Sit at a table when you eat, with the television off.
❑ Attend caregiver support group meetings. (Great place to brainstorm)
❑ Organize yourself, your papers and calendar to avoid frustration.
❑ Be grateful for the times you've enjoyed with your care-receiver in the past, and now.
❑ Take comfort in knowing that you are doing the best you can.
❑ ____
❑ ____

Avoiding Caregiver Burnout I

Tips	I Do It Already	I Don't Because	What Do I Plan to Do
Ex: Exercise everyday	*X*	*I can't leave my care-receiver alone*	*Lift weights while my care-receiver naps*
Ex: Eat and drink healthy	✔		*Continue*
Exercise everyday			
Eat and drink healthy			
Read or listen to a good book			
Go shopping			
Get a manicure, pedicure, massage, etc.			
Use relaxation techniques			
Keep a journal			
Tap into your supports			
Make time for yourself			
Attend a support group			
Ask for and/or accept help			
Say no until you have time			
Make & keep your own doctor appointments			
Take a break from caregiving			
Dream new dreams			
Get enough sleep			
Use your sense of humor			
Practice good self-care			
Have a family meeting when you need to			
Take a relaxing bath or a shower			
Protect your own health			
Stay socially connected			
Ask a friend over for lunch			
Meet religious and/or spiritual needs			
Avoid drugs or alcohol			
Stay involved in your interests			
Find time for YOU			
Go shopping			
Take short naps			
Other			
Other			
Other			

Avoiding Caregiver Burnout II

Problem-Solving

Look at your responses from the *Avoiding Caregiver Burnout's* second column "I DON'T BECAUSE." Pick several you would like to do. On the lines below, list some creative ways to make them happen. Brainstorm with other caregivers for their thoughts and ideas.

Example: **I don't** *read*

because *I have no time*

Problem-solving: *I will listen to an audio book while doing other tasks.*

I don't

because

Problem-solving:

I don't

because

Problem-solving:

I don't

because

Problem-solving:

Finding Meaning in Caregiving

Caregiving can be, and usually is, exhausting – physically and mentally. At some point or other, most caregivers hit a brick wall. Exhaustion and frustration are exacerbated by thoughts such as:
This is too hard. I can't do it anymore.
I don't want to do it anymore. I wish it were over.

What keeps caregivers going when they reach this moment? First, getting the help they need from family, friends, and professionals. Then, turning to their own inner sources of strength. Research shows that caregivers who have a strong faith or whose culture values caregiving are less at risk for depression. For these individuals, their caregiving has a meaning that helps them carry on in difficult times.

The meaning caregivers can find in this challenging task is very personal. As a caregiver, you can find comfort in knowing that what you are doing aligns with your personal, family, cultural and/or spiritual values.

For example:

Love for, and deep commitment to, the care-receiver.

Determination to carry on a family or cultural tradition of caring for others.

Desire to give back to someone who made a difference to you.

Need to express your faith through compassionate caring.

You may also find satisfaction in your accomplishments.

For example:

Performed many daily tasks on behalf of care-receiver.

Learned life-skills in the process.

Advocated in health care issues for the care-receiver.

Role-modeled ways to care for those we love for a younger generation.

The personal growth that can come through caregiving is also a source of strength and self-esteem.

For example:

Ability to keep going in tough times.

Inner strength you may not have known you had before.

Greater insight and understanding of yourself and others.

Deeper feelings of love and compassion.

New sense of what is most important in life.

(Continued on the next page)

Finding Meaning in Caregiving *(Continued)*

How can I find meaning in my caregiving journey?

Use the following questions to help you discover, or rediscover, how your caregiving is an expression of who you are and the values you hold.

1. Have you seen others being cared for in your own family? In other families?
2. How important is it to you to continue this tradition?
3. How has your care-receiver contributed to your life?
4. What difference did it make?
5. What do you hope to contribute to your care-receiver's well-being?
6. What beliefs or values are most important to you?
7. How does caregiving reflect those values or beliefs?
8. How do you feel about yourself, knowing you contribute in this way?
9. Describe your relationship with your care-receiver.
10. How do you feel about yourself, considering the care you are giving your care-receiver?
11. In what ways are you the person who has always stepped up to the plate when action was needed? Explain.
12. What personal characteristics or commitments lead you to do that?
13. How is caregiving an expression of who you are?

(Continued on the next page)

Finding Meaning in Caregiving *(Continued)*

What you have learned by being a caregiver?
Check the statements that apply to you.

1. I have learned …

- ❑ about my care-receiver's illness.
- ❑ practical caregiving skills.
- ❑ how to be my care-receiver's advocate.
- ❑ how to read medical bills.
- ❑ how to navigate the healthcare system.
- ❑ how to use the medical equipment my care-receiver's needs.
- ❑ how to read and understand prescription information.

Other ____

Other ____

Other ____

Other ____

2. About myself, I've discovered I have …

- ❑ patience.
- ❑ inner strength.
- ❑ the ability to find humor in the situation.
- ❑ the ability to let go of old hurts and forgive others and myself.
- ❑ a new sense of what's most important in life.

Other ____

Other ____

Other ____

Other ____

3. About my care-receiver, I've discovered …

- ❑ amazing things I never knew about him or her.
- ❑ his or her inner strength.
- ❑ his or her ability to find humor in the situation.
- ❑ his or her ability to let go of old hurts and forgive.
- ❑ what's important to him or her.

Other ____

Other ____

Other ____

Other ____

Taking Care of Yourself

- **Do what feeds your spirit**

  Examples: Write down five things you're grateful for every day. Attend a religious, spiritual or community event.

  I will____

- **Stay connected to your family and friends**

  Examples: Send cards, e-mails, phone calls.

  I will____

- **Take care of your body**

  Examples: Add more vegetables and fruit to your diet, exercise daily, and attempt to sleep at least 7 hours.

  I will____

- **Ask for the help you need**

  Examples: Your neighbor might be glad to pick up something at the store for you when shopping .

  What can others do for me? ______________________________

  Whom will I call on to do these tasks? ________________________

My Support Network

I NEED SOMEONE WHO WILL . . .	NAME	PHONE	E-MAIL
Talk with Me as a Trusted Friend			
Go Shopping			
Run Errands			
Drive Me Places			
Do Home Repairs			
Stay with Care-Receiver			
Other			

How Can You Help? Well, I Have a Little List!

When most people say, "Let me know if you need anything," they really would like to help. Say yes! Keep a list with you of the things others can do to help you or your care-receiver. Use the list below or write your own. Next time someone says "How can I help?" pull out your list and invite them to choose. You will be doing them a kindness by allowing them to help, and they will be doing the same for you and your situation.

Check off the tasks that would be helpful to you and your care-receiver (CR):

- ❑ Walk the dog
- ❑ Take out the garbage
- ❑ Go food shopping
- ❑ Sit with your CR while you go out
- ❑ Help with the house cleaning
- ❑ Bring a pet to visit
- ❑ Play a game with your CR
- ❑ Do a crossword puzzle with your CR
- ❑ Read a book or magazine to your CR
- ❑ Make phone calls
- ❑ Wash, gas and/or service the car
- ❑ Do gardening or yard work
- ❑ Bring a baby to visit
- ❑ Pick up a take-out dinner or pizza
- ❑ Help with the laundry
- ❑ Do light repairs
- ❑ Pet sit during appointments
- ❑ Listen
- ❑ Bring a cooked meal or dessert
- ❑ Take children for an outing
- ❑ Water the plants
- ❑ Bring a child to sing, dance, etc.
- ❑ Share a hobby with your CR
- ❑ Pick up books from library
- ❑ Return books to library
- ❑ Take CR for a drive
- ❑ Bring an indoor picnic
- ❑ Drive CR to an appointment
- ❑ ____________________
- ❑ ____________________
- ❑ ____________________
- ❑ ____________________
- ❑ ____________________
- ❑ ____________________
- ❑ ____________________
- ❑ ____________________
- ❑ ____________________
- ❑ ____________________
- ❑ ____________________
- ❑ ____________________
- ❑ ____________________
- ❑ ____________________
- ❑ ____________________
- ❑ ____________________
- ❑ ____________________
- ❑ ____________________
- ❑ ____________________
- ❑ ____________________
- ❑ ____________________
- ❑ ____________________

How's Your Stress Level?

The following worksheet will help you become more aware of your current state.

	Seldom True	Sometimes True	Often True	Usually True
I am exhausted				
I don't socialize				
I don't see my family very much				
I cry for no reason or over minor issues				
I have issues with my care-receiver				
I have tension headaches, stomach aches, colds, etc.				
I feel sorry for myself				
I worry about our finances				
I don't get a good night's sleep				
I feel like I don't have enough experience to be a caregiver				
My health is not good				
I don't have any time for myself				
My attitude is not great				
The situation is emotionally draining				
I feel anxious				
I snap at my care-receiver and then feel guilty				
My care-receiver is no longer lovable				
I am afraid to fall asleep and not hear my care-receiver				
I have gained or lost a lot of weight				
I have become short-tempered				
I have given up my hobbies or interests				
I often have outbursts of anger				
I have no time to communicate with or to be with friends				

If the response to more than one or two of these areas is usually true or often true, it may be time for you to arrange for regular respite care so you can have time to take care of yourself.

Creating a Healthy Balance

Sometimes caregivers don't have a clear picture of how well they are balancing caregiving and self-care. This worksheet can help you clarify your situation and develop action items for a healthier you.

What I do daily for my care-receiver	What I do daily for myself
1. ______________________	1. ______________________
2. ______________________	2. ______________________
3. ______________________	3. ______________________
4. ______________________	4. ______________________
5. ______________________	5. ______________________
6. ______________________	6. ______________________
7. ______________________	7. ______________________
8. ______________________	8. ______________________
9. ______________________	9. ______________________
10. ______________________	10. ______________________

How many items are in your care-receiver's "obligations" list? ______________

How many things are on your list? ______________

What does this tell you? ____

____

____

What choices can you make in these areas to help balance caring for another and caring for yourself?

MIND	BODY	SOUL
____________	____________	____________
____________	____________	____________
____________	____________	____________
____________	____________	____________
____________	____________	____________
____________	____________	____________
____________	____________	____________

Think about how this might help both you and your care-receiver.

Just for Today

Just for today … I will ask for help.

Just for today … I will accept help.

Just for today … I will honor my needs.

Just for today … I will take care of myself.

Just for today … I will be patient with myself.

Just for today … I will live through the next twelve hours and not try to tackle all of life's problems at once.

Just for today … I will find something to be grateful for.

Just for today … I will remember what I love about my care-receiver.

Just for today … I will not find fault with my care-receiver.

Just for today … I will not try to change or improve anyone but myself.

Just for today … I will be patient with my care-receiver.

Just for today … I will allow my negative feelings, accept them as they are and move past them.

Just for today … I will forgive myself.

Just for today … I will reach out to others. I don't need to feel alone.

and YOUR ideas are …

Just for today ______________________________

Just for today ______________________________

Just for today ______________________________

Just for today ______________________________

Just for today ______________________________

Just for today ______________________________

Time for Yourself

Doing something to refresh yourself will go a long way to prevent caregiver burnout. Call on friends, family or perhaps a professional to provide respite care. Then use the time to do something just for you, either alone or with people whose company you've been missing.

Check the items in the first column that appeal to you.
In the second column, come up with some ideas of your own.

____ Take a nap.	______________________________
____ See a movie.	______________________________
____ Attend a play or concert.	______________________________
____ Shop and have lunch with friends.	______________________________
____ Run errands.	______________________________
____ Make and keep your own healthcare appointments.	______________________________
____ Enjoy a massage.	______________________________
____ See your financial advisor.	______________________________
____ Go to club to which you belong.	______________________________
____ Take a class.	______________________________
____ Write notes, e-mails or letters.	______________________________
____ Have a good night's sleep.	______________________________
____ Attend a caregiver's support group.	______________________________
____ Practice a craft you enjoy.	______________________________
____ Treat yourself to a manicure or pedicure.	______________________________
____ Confide in a trusted friend.	______________________________
____Take a walk, hike, bicycle ride outdoors.	______________________________
____ Read a magazine article.	______________________________
____ Attend a house of worship.	______________________________
____ Confer with a religious or spiritual advisor.	______________________________
____ Exercise.	______________________________
____ Solve a crossword, jigsaw, Sudoku or any other puzzle.	______________________________
____ Enjoy a cup of coffee or tea at a sidewalk cafe.	______________________________
____ Use deep breathing and/or relaxation exercises.	______________________________

Creative Time Management

Since time is precious to caregivers, being creative is the way to go! When your care-receiver is doing something that requires you to be right there, use that time effectively by organizing and planning ahead. This will allow you to have a sense of accomplishment, be more patient and feel grateful that you have been alongside your care-receiver.

Think outside of the box! In the blank boxes on the left, write your care-receiver's activities. On the opposite side, write what you may do at the same time. Be creative.

Your Care-Receiver is ...	At the same time you can ...
Example: Taking a walk – very slowly	*Exercise by walking backwards*
Example: Waiting at the doctor's office	*Balance your checkbook, do a crossword puzzle*
Taking a walk – very slowly	
Waiting at the doctor's office	
Getting dressed	
Eating breakfast	
Doing physical or occupational therapy	
Watching television	
In the emergency room or hospital	

What I Did for Myself Today

I am making a commitment to do something special for myself every day, even if it's simply taking a walk around the block, meditating or enjoying cup of flavored coffee or herbal tea.

Signed ____________________________

MONTH ____________________

1) ____________________
2) ____________________
3) ____________________
4) ____________________
5) ____________________
6) ____________________
7) ____________________
8) ____________________
9) ____________________
10) ____________________
11) ____________________
12) ____________________
13) ____________________
14) ____________________
15) ____________________
16) ____________________
17) ____________________
18) ____________________
19) ____________________
20) ____________________
21) ____________________
22) ____________________
23) ____________________
24) ____________________
25) ____________________
26) ____________________
27) ____________________
28) ____________________
29) ____________________
30) ____________________
31) ____________________

Your Private Journal

**You may be a good caregiver,
but you are not a Superwoman or Superman!**

The stress of caregiving brings up feelings and thoughts that may be shocking to you. For example,

I just wish this were over.
Sometimes I feel like running away.
I don't care what happens.

Such feelings make caregivers feel guilty, not good enough and ashamed. They tend to stuff those feelings, which adds significantly to caregiver stress. The best way to handle them is to express them at appropriate time and/or place.

A caregiver support group is a good place to vent, but it may not be available at the time you're on the edge of a meltdown. For those moments when you need to get something off your chest *right now*; the safest way to do that is to journal.

How private is private?

When beginning a journal, take a moment to think about how revealing you wish to be. Will you be writing a *burn at my death* journal, one in which you say exactly how you feel, with no holding back?

If so, you need to take steps to ensure no one will ever read it. Have a safe place to store it when you are not using it. If you have a small, locked security box, give a second key to someone you trust, with the understanding that the journal will be destroyed if anything should happen to you.

If you don't feel confident your boundaries will be honored, you may opt to pull back a little, alluding to happenings or feelings rather than being explicit about them. You will find value in journaling even if you do edit yourself as you write.

Journaling can help you deal with …

- What's happening to the care-receiver, changes in personality, etc.
- Feelings of loss, grief, regret, etc.
- Fear of the future
- Your own impatience and attitude
- Anger and resentment toward the care-receiver and perhaps family members
- Depression, sadness
- Problem solving
- Gaining clarity
- Decision making

Journaling – How to Begin

Some people are natural journal writers. They put pen to paper and the words flow. Others don't find it as easy. When they look at an empty page, their mind goes blank, or they fear acknowledging how they really feel on paper.

Gratitude journals are popular because they offer a way to begin:

Today I am grateful ____.

A plus of the gratitude journal is that you can write anything! You are encouraged to write the truth – good, bad or ugly.

For example: *Today, I am grateful for sunshine and flowers.*

A harried mother might write, *Today I am grateful that I didn't yell at my kids.*

Here are some starters for a caregiver journal entry:

1. Today was ____
2. Today I (*an action or thought you wouldn't tell anyone*) ____________________
3. On a scale of 1–10, with ten being at the end of my rope, right now I'm ____________________

   because ____

   ____

Other prompts to get you writing:

I wish ____

I remember ____

I think ____

If I could change anything, I ____

I wish I could tell ____

I feel ____

Sometimes I wonder if ____

I hope ____

I want ____

I need ____

Communication

CHAPTER 4

Caregivers are challenged to communicate effectively in difficult or emotionally charged situations. This chapter includes sections on basic communication, how to communicate when the care-receiver is confused or difficult to work with, and how to be more empathetic. It concludes with a section on preparing for and having sensitive conversations.

15 Reminders of Effective Communication Principles

1. Check to see if your care-receiver has on glasses and hearing aids.
2. Look at your care-receiver when he or she is speaking.
   Be aware of non-verbal communication.
3. Answer all of your care-receiver's questions. Don't rush.
4. Imagine yourself in your care-receiver's world.
   How would you feel in his or her situation?
5. Speak to your care-receiver as one adult to another. Use a respectful tone.
6. Acknowledge your care-receiver's objections and concerns.
7. Allow your care-receiver time to absorb what you're saying.
   Clarify or state in a different way if necessary. Offer options.
8. Mirror back what you think you've heard your care-receiver say. Ask questions.
9. Stay calm. Don't take anything personally.
10. Give your care-receiver time to think things over.
    Don't press for an immediate answer.
11. Think of this as a time to get to know your care-receiver better.
    Listen for concerns and fears. What would give him or her comfort?
    With whom would he or she like to talk?
12. Take a break if your care-receiver is tired or either of you becomes upset.
    Return to the conversation at an appropriate time.
13. Make sure you have heard your care-receiver's decision correctly and are interpreting it as intended.
14. Request help from other family members if necessary and/or appropriate.
    See *A Meeting of the Minds*, pages 106–110.
15. Remember, you are not alone. There are two of you in the equation.
    Keep communications open.

Stop, Look and Listen!
Steps to Effective Communication

The ability to express ourselves clearly and to understand what others are trying to say to us, is the key to success in all areas of our lives. Most of us have not been trained in the principles of good communication. We do not always listen to what is being said. Instead we are busy formulating and justifying our own point of view. We also become derailed by bringing up the past, especially old hurts and resentments.

If we had taken a communication class, it would likely have had two parts:

Part I. How to really hear – and really understand – what others are saying
Part II. How to express feelings and thoughts without dragging in past conflicts and emotions

It takes commitment and practice to improve communication with your care-receiver, medical team, family members, etc. You can begin by noticing when you are on automatic and then remembering what you learned about crossing a street safely: Stop, Look and Listen.

Part I – Listening

A. Stop what you're doing. *Be present, eliminate distractions, stop talking, etc.*

B. Look at the speaker. *Give full attention; notice body-language.*

C. Listen to what is being said. *Allow speaker time to finish, don't jump to conclusions.*

D. Double check. *Be certain you have all the facts, ask for more information if needed.*

Once you have done all the above, is it your turn and time to express your thoughts and feelings.

Part II – Your turn to speak

A. "Be" Attitudes

- Be focused. *Address the issue at hand. Do not bring strong emotions and issues from the past into the discussion.*
- Be specific. *Do not assume the listener knows what you're thinking. Offer clarification if necessary.*
- Be calm. *If the speaker is distraught, be calm. If you are in an emotional state where you are unable to discuss an issue, agree to continue the discussion later.*
- Be polite. *Do not use inflammatory words. Avoid insults and accusations. They will lead to a heated argument and make the problem worse.*

B. When pointing out an existing problem

- Identify the issue without blaming or shaming. *Avoid personal attacks.*
- Use "I" statements. *"I feel ___________________, when you ___________________."*
- Offer solutions as preferences. *"I would prefer it if you (we) ___________________.*

C. Make allowances if the other person has hearing or vision loss, or is confused.
(see page 88, *Compassionate Communication*).

D. Revisit the issue if you cannot reach a consensus.
Accept the fact that there are some problems for which there are no solutions.

What Keeps Me From Being a Better Listener?

Your ability to be empathetic, compassionate and loving depends a great deal on how you are feeling at the moment. This is especially true when your situation seems more difficult than usual. If you are feeling overwhelmed and find yourself being short and impatient with your care-receiver and others, it is time to take stock of what is going on within you.

Check the sentences that apply to you and then problem-solve under each statement how you can remedy the situation. If you need suggestions, brainstorm with others.

I could listen better if . . .

- ❑ I had more sleep

  ____

- ❑ I had someone I could talk to and get things off my chest.

  ____

- ❑ I felt appreciated by my care-receiver and/or supported by family members.

  ____

- ❑ I did not have so many things to do for my care-receiver.

  ____

- ❑ I did not have so many household, financial and other chores of my own.

  ____

- ❑ I did not feel so angry. This is not how I thought my life would be.

  ____

- ❑ I did not feel guilty for wishing the situation or my care-receiver was different.

  ____

- ❑ I did not also have to work or take care of my own children and/or spouse.

  ____

- ❑ I had a day off.

  ____

- ❑ I was not so depressed.

  ____

- ❑ I was not dealing with health issues of my own.

  ____

- ❑ I felt others recognized that my needs are important, too.

  ____

In the future, when ______________________________ happens,
I will ______________________________.

In the future, when ______________________________ happens,
I will ______________________________.

Compassionate Communication

with a care-receiver who is confused or easily overwhelmed by a lot of information.

Preparation

- Eliminate or reduce background noise.
- If care-receiver uses hearing aids, make sure they are in and functioning properly.
- If care-receiver wears glasses, make sure they are on.

Style of Speaking

- Address your care-receiver by name, looking directly at him or her.
- Maintain eye contact to help keep your care-receiver's attention.
- Use simple words and short sentences.
- Speak slowly and clearly in a moderate voice.
- Keep your tone of voice calm and caring.

Help your care-receiver to understand

- Allow time for your care-receiver to process your words and respond to them.
- Repeat the sentence if necessary, but not louder unless he or she is hearing impaired. If he or she still doesn't understand, try restating your question in different words.
- Use questions that can be answered yes or no, or give the person two choices.
  DO: *Do you want chicken or fish for supper?* ***DON'T:*** *What do you want for supper?*
- Break tasks into single steps and then ask care-receiver to take one at a time.
- List the steps on a chart or use flash cards with words and/or pictures. Keep them simple. Use large, bold print.

Make sure you understand what your care-receiver intends to communicate

- Mirror back what you have heard so your care-receiver can clarify, if necessary.
- Pay attention to non-verbal communication.

Support your care-receiver emotionally

- Show affection with praise, hugs and hand-holding.
- Be calm and reassuring.
- Be consistent.
- If dementia is an issue, do not argue, disagree or try to prove the care-receiver is wrong and you're right. Whatever the care-receiver has said, he or she is absolutely right in his or her world.
- Use humor, but never by making fun of the care-receiver.
- If you are both frustrated, change the topic or involve your care-receiver in a task he or she can do. If the communication is necessary, try again later.

Establish a routine

- Organize daily activities as much as possible.
- Place eyeglasses, hearing aids, and TV remote in the same place every day. Label location, if necessary.
- Place a large calendar in a central location. Review it with your care-receiver daily, ideally in the morning, to establish a plan for the day's activities. Some people like using a white-board and writing the day's activities together each morning. Consider marking complete tasks with a star.
- Use an alarm as a medication alert, especially if your care-receiver's medication schedule is complicated. Some pill containers have a built-in alarm. A watch with a programmable alarm or the alarm on a cell phone also works well.

What other tips can you and others share?

Communication with a KISS

Keep **I**t **S**hort and **S**imple

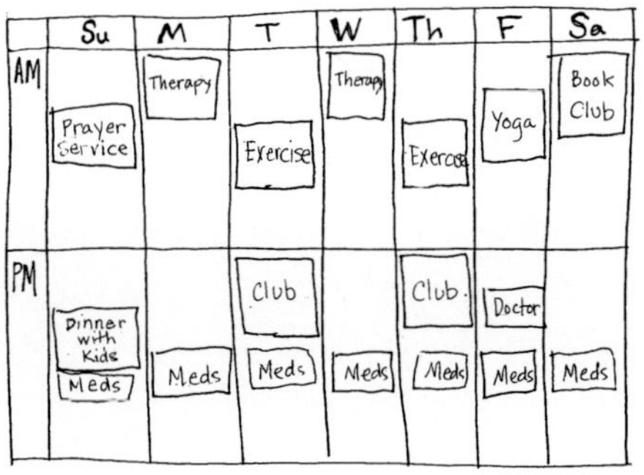

	Su	M	T	W	Th	F	Sa
AM	Prayer Service	Therapy	Exercise	Therapy	Exercise	Yoga	Book Club
PM	Dinner with Kids / Meds	Meds	Club / Meds	Meds	Club / Meds	Doctor / Meds	Meds

How to give simple instructions to the confused:

1. Pick a task that your care-receiver is having trouble beginning or completing.

   ____

   ____

2. Break the task into small, easy-to-do steps.

   ____

   ____

   ____

3. If it would be helpful, create flash cards with simple words or illustrations. (Cut out pictures or words from a magazine and tape them on index cards.) What type of flash cards would help your care-receiver?

   ____

   ____

   ____

   ____

The Value of a Daily Chart

Care-receivers experiencing some degree of memory loss or confusion will benefit from a daily chart large enough to be easily read and posted in a prime location. Looking at it can help them orient themselves to what day it is, their usual activities and any non-routine activities that have been scheduled.

Here is one way of making a daily chart

- Buy an erasable whiteboard to put on the refrigerator or a cabinet door.
- Create a grid on it listing the days of the week across the top, with sections for morning, afternoon and evening underneath. You may wish to do this with a permanent marker.
- Using erasable markers, outline each day with as many details as necessary.
  Example: Rise, bathroom, dress, breakfast, medicines, favorite TV show, nap, etc.
- Add appointments and other special events in a different color.
  Example: Home healthcare provider visit, doctor's appointment, hair cut, visitors.

Review the activities of the day at the same time every morning, when your care-receiver is most alert. Refer to it again if your care-receiver feels lost or is confused about what's happening and why.

Listening Skills Checklist

Place a check (✔) if you believe the statement is true for you, with your care-receiver.
Place a dash (–) by the statement if it is sometimes true for you, with your care-receiver.
Place an (X) if the statement is not true for you, with your care-receiver.

_____ 1. I am able to completely focus and not think about anything else when listening to my care-receiver.

_____ 2. I make eye-contact with my care-receiver when he/she is speaking.

_____ 3. My body language (a smile, a nod, touch) encourages my care-receiver to speak.

_____ 4. I ignore all distractions around us.

_____ 5. If my care-receiver hesitates or loses his or her train of thought, I patiently encourage him or her to continue.

_____ 6. I listen without interrupting, even if I can anticipate what my care-receiver is going to say.

_____ 7. I concentrate on understanding the message my care-receiver is trying to communicate.

_____ 8. I listen and am sensitive to the feelings of my care-receiver.

_____ 9. I sometimes question my care-receiver to be sure I understand.

_____ 10. I reflect or paraphrase what my care-receiver has said to be sure I understand.

_____ 11. I check out my care-receiver's feelings by asking for clarification. *"You seem upset. Can you tell me what's bothering you?"*

_____ 12. I am comfortable with silence between us.

_____ 13. I am able to listen without judgment when my care-receiver says something negative about how he or she is feeling. I appreciate the honesty.

Look over your responses and note the listening skills which you are proud of and those you would like to improve.

I'm proud of . . .	**I would like to improve . . .**
______________________	______________________
______________________	______________________
______________________	______________________
______________________	______________________
______________________	______________________

Entering Your Care-Receiver's World

Emotions can run high in a care-giving situation.
It's the way people often react when they are under stress.

STRESS + EMOTIONS =
MISUNDERSTANDINGS AND/OR BLOWUPS

You may be able to avoid unpleasant scenes with a conscious commitment to enter your care-receiver's reality. Doing so increases empathy and understanding, which are crucial to meaningful communication. Think of it as learning a skill that will improve your interactions with others now and in the future.

You can go through this worksheet as a reminder any time you need to shift or calm your reaction to the person you care for.

1. **Walk around the block in your care-receiver's shoes.** What is it like to be that person today?

____

____

2. **Listen to the feelings behind your care-recipient's words.** What do or could you say to acknowledge them? *("You sound like you're feeling sad." or, "I can see this is frustrating for you.")*

____

____

3. **Pay attention to your care-receiver's body language.** What does that language tell you? Is it different from the care-receiver's words?

____

____

4. **Down-shift to a pace that matches your care-receiver's.** What can you do to remain calm and patient while waiting for him or her to do something you could do much more quickly?

____

____

5. **Resist the urge to correct your care-receiver or tell him or her not to feel that way.** What can you do or say instead?

____

____

What technique can you use to stay centered and compassionate?
(For example: Count to 10, breathe deeply, use the Emotional Freedom Technique, recite the Serenity Prayer, etc.)

Listen, Please

Author Unknown

Write the name of your care-receiver. ______________________________
Imagine your care-receiver reading this to you.

When I ask you to listen to me
  and you start giving advice,
  you have not done what I asked
  nor heard what I need.

When I ask you to listen to me
  and you begin to tell me why I shouldn't feel that way,
  you are trampling on my feelings.

When I ask you to listen to me
  and you feel you have to do something to solve my problems,
  you have failed me - strange as that may seem.

Listen, please!
  All I asked was that you listen.
  Not talk nor "do" - just hear me.
  Advice is cheap. The newspaper will get me "Dear Abby"
  And that I can read for myself.

I'm not helpless. Maybe discouraged and faltering, but not helpless.
  When you do something for me that I can and need to do for myself,
  You contribute to my fear and weakness.

But when you accept as a simple fact that I do feel what I feel,
  then I can quit trying to convince you
  and get about the business of understanding
  what's behind this feeling.

Feelings make sense when we understand what's behind them.
  Perhaps that's why, for some people, prayer or meditation works.

So, please listen and just hear me.
  And if you want to talk, wait until it's your turn,
  and I promise I'll listen to you.

How do you think your care-receiver would react or relate to this poem? Would he or she feel this way?

____

____

Describe a time when you felt the same way as the author of this poem.

____

____

How are we doing? A Reality Check for Care-Partners

For the CAREGIVER

Complete this page on your own and ask your care-receiver to complete the corresponding page on his/her own, if able.

If possible, come together afterwards and compare responses and perceptions.

In what areas are your answers similar?

In what areas are they different?

What changes might you make based on your answers?

1. What are your major concerns at the moment? ______________________________
____
2. Have you shared these concerns with your care-receiver? Yes _____ No _____ Some_____
3. If no, explain.
4. Have you shared them with someone else? Yes _____ No _____ Some_____
5. If yes, explain. ____
6. Do you have emotions or thoughts that you hold back from your care-receiver?
Yes _____ No _____ Some_____
7. If yes, explain. ____
____
8. Do you share these emotions or thoughts with anyone? Yes _____ No _____ Some_____
9. If yes, explain.
10. How do you handle these thoughts and emotions?______________________________
____
11. Do you believe your care-receiver knows how you are feeling right now?
Yes _____ No _____ Some_____
12. Do you believe you understand your care-receiver's wishes regarding medical emergencies and Living Will issues? Yes _____ No _____ Some_____
13. Do you think your family members have a clear understanding of your current situation?
Yes _____ No _____ Some _____
14. Is there something you would like to tell your care-receiver, but haven't? What is it? ____________
____
15. Can you find a way of saying what you would like to say that might work out well for both of you? How?
____

How are we doing? A Reality Check for Care Partners

For the CARE-RECEIVER

Once you have completed this page, come together with your caregiver and compare responses and perceptions.

In what areas are your answers similar?

In what areas are they different?

What changes might you make based on your answers?

1. What are your major concerns at the moment? ____________________

    ____
2. Have you shared these concerns with your care-receiver? Yes _____ No _____ Some_____
3. If yes, explain.
4. Have you shared them with someone else? Yes _____ No _____ Some_____
5. If no, explain.____________________
6. Do you have emotions or thoughts that you hold back from your care-receiver?

    Yes _____ No _____ Some_____
7. If yes, explain. ____________________

    ____
8. Do you share these emotions or thoughts with anyone? Yes _____ No _____ Some_____
9. If yes, explain.
10. How do you handle these thoughts and emotions?____________________

    ____
11. Do you believe your care-receiver knows how you are feeling right now?

    Yes _____ No _____ Some_____
12. Do you believe you understand your care-receiver's wishes regarding medical emergencies and Living Will issues? Yes _____ No _____ Some_____
13. Do you think your family members have a clear understanding of your current situation?

    Yes _____ No _____ Some _____
14. Is there something you would like to tell your care-receiver, but haven't? What is it? ____________________

    ____
15. Can you find a way of saying what you would like to say that might work out well for both of you? How?

    ____

Coping with Difficult Behavior

Caregiving is a challenge especially if your care-receiver is short-tempered, resists your help, and/or uses rude or abusive language.

If that behavior is intermittent, you might feel able to handle the situation. However, if your care-receiver is consistently inconsiderate or abusive, you will want to look for possible causes. Understanding what's behind such behavior can help you create strategies for handling the situation, although not all difficult behavior is explainable or solvable.

Possible Causes of Difficult Behavior

1. Over-medication or Adverse Drug Reaction

Many people who are ill see a number of different physicians, all of whom write them prescriptions. This can result in an individual using medications that have overlapping actions and/or side effects, that should never be used in combination, or that were once prescribed for a condition that no longer exists.

Over-medication or an adverse drug reaction can cause changes in mood, cognitive function and behavior. If your care-receiver's behavior has changed markedly from what it has been in the past, make a list of all of the supplements, prescriptions and over-the-counter medicines that he or she uses. Then ask his or her primary care physician or pharmacist to review it. Using the same pharmacy for all prescriptions is advisable.

Even if this review does not explain your care-receiver's behavior, having done it may give you confidence that you're doing the best you can for your care-receiver.

2. Changes in Ability to See or Hear

Loss of vision or hearing can occur so slowly that individuals may not realize why they are having trouble understanding what is going on around them. Instead of admitting they do not understand and asking for clarification, they may react with anger born of fear. If your care-receiver's vision and hearing haven't been checked recently, schedule appointments. A new pair of glasses or a hearing aid may help your care-receiver feel less anxious.

3. Pain, Hunger or Lack of Restorative Sleep

Many conditions can cause a care-receiver pain. Be alert for signs, both verbal or non-verbal, that he or she is uncomfortable. Use both the prescribed medications and non-drug alternative methods to provide pain relief.

Hunger and lack of restorative sleep can make a healthy person irritable and impatient - and an ill person even more so. Hunger can be addressed by providing regular meals and small snacks, and being watchful for indications that your care-receiver needs to eat. In the section, *Helping Myself with Healthy Habits* see *Simple Steps to Healthy Eating*, page 64, and *Helping Myself with Restful Sleep*, page 65.

(Continued on the next page)

Possible Causes for Difficult Behavior *(Continued)*

4. Over-Stimulation

Exposure to substances or situations that over-stimulate a care-receiver can make him or her short-tempered or anxious. Watch for reactions following these or similar situations:

- Excessive caffeine intake
- TV shows or movies with lots of action and suspense or disturbing themes
- Radio or TV on all the time
- Continual use of computer games
- Too many visitors at once
- Constant visitors, allowing little 'alone time'

5. Major life changes

Individuals who are becoming increasingly dependent upon others due to age, illness and/or disability, or who have recently received a negative prognosis, can understandably feel they are losing control over their lives. They may react with anger, fear and resentment. Rude and/or demanding behavior can be their way of maintaining a semblance of, if not actual, control.

You, as the caregiver, often bear the brunt of these negative emotions. Encourage your care-receiver to talk about concerns, whether to you, a therapist or someone trusted with whom the person can talk freely. Not only will he or she feel better, you may gain a new understanding of the reasons for the outbursts. Putting yourself in his or her shoes can help you be more patient and compassionate.

6. Financial worries

There are many reasons why care-receivers worry about money issues: concern over adequate funds, loss of ability to balance their own checkbook and manage their own finances.

Frank communication can allay some of these fears in this regard. If you or someone else have taken over your care-receiver's finances, explain what is happening with monthly expenses. Also include him or her in family financial planning sessions if he or she is able to understand the issues.

Look for patterns in your care-receiver's behavior

As you read the information above, you may have had some insight into your care-receiver's behavior. Consider these observations as you work through the following pages to identify recurring patterns, and possible solutions.

My Insights into My Care-Receiver's Behavior

1. **My care-receiver tends to get angry, upset, or frustrated**

   a. **In the** ❑ morning ❑ afternoon ❑ evening ❑ ____________

   b. ✷❇❈■ ❇❈ ❑❒ ▲❇❈ ❉▲ ❑ bored ❑ tired ❑ hungry ❑ ____________

   c. **When he or she** ❑ has had a bad night ❑ is in pain ❑ ____________

   d. **When** ❑ we go shopping ❑ we go for a walk ❑ he or she gets ready for bed
   ❑ we're talking about ____________
   ❑ ____________

   e. **When** ❑ I ask him or her to ____________

   f. **When** ❑ I have someone else come in to provide care
   ❑ I have someone else come in to stay while I go out for a while
   ❑ ____________ comes to visit

   g. **After watching this program on television** ❑ ____________
   ❑ ____________

   h. **Other** ____________
   ____
   ____

2. **In general what patterns are staying the same? What patterns are getting worse?** ____________
____
____

3. **Is there a time when things are better?** ____________
____
____

4. **What makes the difference?** ____________
____
____

5. **What can you do to improve communications, and thus interactions, between you and your care-receiver in each of the situations addressed in #1 above?**
____
____
____

My Behavior as a Caregiver

It may be tempting to put the blame for unpleasantness on the care-receiver, especially if he or she has a history of being difficult. However, if you make him or her totally responsible for what is happening, then you also make him or her totally responsible for the solution.

On the other hand, if you acknowledge that your emotions and behavior also contribute to the situation, you are in a position to come up with action steps that can make a difference for both of you. Answering the following questions may give you ideas about where to start.

About Me

A. 1. How often do you experience the following emotions?

Check the box that is most accurate.

I feel angry	❑ rarely	❑ sometimes	❑ often	❑ all the time
I feel exhausted	❑ rarely	❑ sometimes	❑ often	❑ all the time
I feel frustrated	❑ rarely	❑ sometimes	❑ often	❑ all the time
I feel overwhelmed	❑ rarely	❑ sometimes	❑ often	❑ all the time
I feel resentful	❑ rarely	❑ sometimes	❑ often	❑ all the time
I feel unappreciated	❑ rarely	❑ sometimes	❑ often	❑ all the time

2. When do you tend to have a short fuse?

a. **In the** ❑ morning ❑ afternoon ❑ evening ❑ ____________________

b. **When I'm** ❑ tired ❑ hungry ❑ lonely ❑ worried about the future
❑ feeling sorry for myself ❑ ______________________________

c. **When** ❑ I have had a bad night ❑ my care-receiver has had a bad night

d. **When my care-receiver** ❑ is ______________________________
❑ does ______________________________
❑ behaves ______________________________

3. What are some of your other hot buttons?

Ex: I get frustrated at how slowly my care-receiver moves.

I get frustrated ______________________________.

I get angry ______________________________.

I get impatient ______________________________.

I'm resentful ______________________________.

I feel guilty ______________________________.

I hate ______________________________.

(Continued on the next page)

My Behavior as a Caregiver *(Continued)*

4. What do you wish were different?

I wish I had__________

I wish I could __________

I wish I didn't feel guilty about __________

5. What do you fear?

I am afraid __________

because I__________

B. Rate your self-care

What are you doing to take care of your own emotional health? __________

What are you doing to take care of your own physical health? __________

How are you fulfilling your own social and spiritual needs? __________

Whom do you call upon for support? __________

What can you do to improve your current situation?__________

(Continued on the next page)

My Behavior as a Caregiver *(Continued)*

C. What have you learned about yourself?
Use the space below to describe your insights.

Steps You Can Take Now

1. **Don't take your care-receiver's behavior personally.** Act rather than react by planning now how you will handle hot-button issues. Avoid subjects or activities you know will end in unpleasantness. Divert attention from the subject with the choice of other activities. Walk away if necessary.
2. **Set boundaries and stick to them.** For example, if you are no longer willing to tolerate name-calling or other degrading behaviors, say so in calm, factual words. Walk away if the behavior persists.
3. **Pick your battles.** Not every irritation is worth a confrontation. Decide what behaviors you can let slide and focus on the issues that are significant.
4. **Avoid name-calling, put-downs, and inflammatory language.** Rather than using the language of blame, use "I statements." For example, instead of, *"You hurt my feelings,"* try saying, *"I feel hurt when you talk that way."*
5. **Strive to understand your care-receiver.** Recognize that requests you might think are frivolous are important to him or her. Acknowledge your care-receiver's frustrations. Ask him to explain what he's feeling. *"You seem ___________. Can you tell me why? Do you want my help?"*
6. **When your care-receiver is upset, arguing accomplishes nothing.** Find ways to agree and validate him or her. Care-receiver: *"These eggs are too hard. I like them over easy."*
You: *"You're right, I let them cook too long."*
7. **Give him or her opportunities to be in control.** Whenever possible, allow your care-receiver to make decisions. If he or she is confused, offer only two options.
8. **Take care of yourself.** Look at your answers in part B and write ways you can take care of yourself in the upcoming week.

a. ____

b. ____

c. ____

Touchy Topics, Sensitive Conversations

As a caregiver, you will likely need to talk to your care-receiver about topics you would rather avoid. Your care-receiver may also wish to avoid them. But this can create problems down the line.

Some examples of touchy topics:

- Loss of physical functions (need to wear protective garments)
- Loss of mental functions (inability to do tasks that were formerly easy)
- Loss of independence (give up driving, need assistance with bathing, dressing)
- Bad news (change in prognosis, prospect of going into assisted living or a nursing facility)
- Finances (not enough money to pay for home healthcare aide or other needs)
- The need for a will, power of attorney, and advance directives for end-of-life issues

Caregivers and family members may put off these sensitive conversations to avoid conflict or the feelings of loss, grief or regret that can come up during such discussions. They may have the erroneous belief that silence protects the care-receiver and others involved, or they just may avoid dealing with pertinent issues by putting their heads in the sand.

If you are resisting such a conversation, consider the benefits of having frank discussions about care issues. They include reduced stress from taking care of something that was hovering over you; clarity regarding care-receiver's feelings and wishes and being able to make plans for the future. You and your care-receiver may also feel the increased closeness that can come through the sharing of values, feelings and memories.

Your approach as a caregiver makes all of the difference. Here are some tips to keep in mind …

- State the issue and possible solutions in a neutral way.
- Discuss, do not debate the issue.
- Realize several conversations will likely be needed.
- Look for points of agreement.
- Respect your care-receiver's right to choose.
- Honor his or her perceptions, beliefs and values.
- Be honest, but kind, in your communication.
- Keep the issues in perspective and the person in mind.
- Remember how you would like to be treated if you were the care-receiver.

If the care-receiver is confused, allow him or her to set the pace. Maintain his or her dignity by offering two choices, if feasible and appropriate. In cases where the care-receiver's safety is the issue, caregivers may need to make the decisions unilaterally.

Remember that you are having this conversation with your care-receiver because you care about his or her well-being and future.

Preparing for Sensitive Conversations

Are you clear about why the conversation is necessary? Before initiating a conversation about an important issue, take time to think about what you want to say, how the other person might react, and the desired result. The following questions will help you know if you are ready to address the issue(s).

What is an issue you feel you need to discuss with your care-receiver? ______________________

____

Why are you having this conversation?

Why is it important to have this conversation now? ______________________

What outcome do you hope to achieve? ______________________

How does the outcome benefit your care-receiver? ______________________

How does this outcome benefit you?______________________

Have you prepared to have the conversation?

Have you studied available information on the topic in question? ______________________

What research have you done? ______________________

What are your concerns? State them without sounding accusatory. ______________________

____

____

Clearly state the solution you want the care-receiver to consider, giving the person a few choices, even if they seem insignificant. ______________________

____

If appropriate and/or necessary, have you discussed the issue with other family members or friends? How did that work out? ______________________

____

How supportive are your family members with your approach to the problem and the solution you mean to suggest? ______________________

____

If you do not feel you have strong support, what steps are you taking to get other family members on board?

____

____

How prepared emotionally are you to discuss the issue?______________________

____

Plan When and How You Will Have the Conversation

When and how you bring up an important issue can affect how beneficial the conversation is to both you and your care-receiver. Worry about an issue, and concern about how a conversation may proceed, can cause caregivers to lose sight of common-sense steps such as the following:

DOs

- Do address an issue when it first comes up so you can talk about it more than once.
- Do find a time when your care-receiver is most alert.
- Do be sure that your care-receiver feels as good as possible physically.
- Do be sure that your care-receiver feels emotionally the best he or she can be.
- Do be sure that you feel rested and alert.
- Do be sure you feel positive, patient and loving.
- Do take it slowly, easily and gently.
- Do give your care-receiver time to think.

DON'Ts

- Don't bring the subject up in the evening or when you know your care-receiver is tired.
- Don't bring it up if your care-receiver is not feeling well.
- Don't bring it up if you have just had an argument or either one of you is upset for any reason.
- Don't bring it up when you are tired, headachy, frustrated or angry.
- Don't bring it up just before you are going to have visitors.
- Don't bring it up right before you have to go somewhere. Once you start the conversation, you want to have sufficient time to discuss it as much as your care-receiver desires so that he or she does not feel rushed and/or manipulated.
- Don't bring it up when you have a chance of being interrupted.

When is my care-receiver most alert? ____________________

When does my care-receiver feel the best physically? ____________________

When does my care-receiver feel the best emotionally? ____________________

When am I feeling the most alert and rested? ____________________

When am I most likely to feel positive and loving? ____________________

Finally, cut both your care-receiver and yourself some slack.

Even if you have done everything you can to prepare for a sensitive conversation and you are in a solid emotional state, it may not turn out the way you hoped. You may have to back off and start again more than once. Both of you may need to apologize for an overheated reaction. But if you and your care-receiver are talking, you are taking perhaps the single most important step you can to ensure his or her future wellbeing.

Family & Close Friend Dynamics

CHAPTER **5**

To be effective, caregiving must involve others beyond the primary caregiver. This includes family members, whether near or far away, and/or other concerned individuals. This chapter guides the caregiver on how to conduct family meetings, discuss the care-receiver's current health, address finances and end-of-life issues, and ask for the help necessary to avoid burnout. Ideas are also generated for handling the holidays and visits to the care-receiver.

I will let love flow

I allow myself to feel my emotions. I express them appropriately.

I make time to keep up with relationships.

I seek help and accept it with gratitude.

I work with my care-receiver, family and close friends to find meaning in the challenges we face.

I draw on positive experiences from our past to sustain me.

No matter how overwhelmed we are, I will find at least one positive thing to focus on.

Even in the worst of times, I will let love flow.

A Meeting of the Minds
with Family and/or Close-Friends

If you are a family member or close friend caring for an aging parent, spouse, child, close relative or friend, you probably know by now that you cannot do this alone. You need help and support.

You may already be having informal conversations via telephone, e-mail or in person, where you inform people of what is happening with your care-receiver. This can be effective in the beginning. As your care-receiver's condition worsens and the burden of his or her care becomes greater, a more formal family and/or close-friend meeting is important. If there are long-distance relatives and friends involved, consider including them. This will enable you to create a good working relationship, before the issues you're facing become complex. These relationships will be when dealing with future issues and concerns.

A family and/or close-friend meeting offers everyone involved the opportunity to …

- Talk about feelings and concerns.
- Hear your report on the current situation.
- Brainstorm ways to solve problems.
- Share the caregiving burden (even those living far away can help and be supportive).
- Begin the conversation about future needs as your care-receiver's situation worsens.

You may be hesitant to call a family and/or close-friend meeting for a variety of reasons.

Do any of these statements sound like something you might hear or say?

- *"My family? Forget it. We'd just end up arguing."*
- *"Everyone has their own problems to deal with."*
- *"My care-receiver has alienated everyone. Nobody cares about him or her."*
- *"The men in my family are uncomfortable talking about certain aspects of caregiving."*
- *"My family and good friends are scattered all over the country. We'd never get everyone together at the same time."*

Thanks to modern technology, distance is no longer a barrier. Family meetings can be effectively conducted via conference calls or an online service that enables voice and video phone calls over the Internet.

Despite any obstacles, it is important that close relatives and friends are informed of the current status of your care-receiver. They need to realize what you are dealing with every day, and ways they can help and support you. It is far better for them to be informed all along than receive urgent phone calls later.

(Continued on the next page)

A Meeting of the Minds with Family and/or Close-Friends

(Continued)

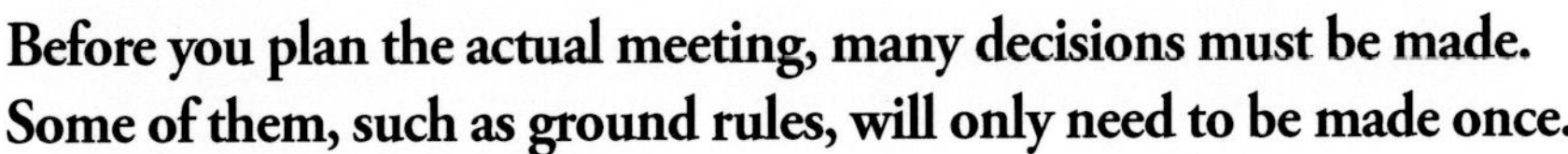

Before you plan the actual meeting, many decisions must be made. Some of them, such as ground rules, will only need to be made once.

1. **Who should be present?**

   By definition, this meeting is for the care-receiver's family members. It can also include close friends and others, depending on the care-receiver's situation and the focus of the meeting.

   - Will you be exploring how to pay for home health care?
     Invite family members and very close friends only.
   - Will you be asking others to help with caregiving tasks?
     You might include neighbors, friends and members of the care-receiver's local, religious or spiritual community who are willing to help.
   - Will you be discussing the care-receiver's worsening condition and planning for his or her future needs?
     Including a case manager or social worker would be helpful.
   - Do you anticipate being unable to agree on crucial matters pertaining to the care-receiver's care?
     You may want to include a mediator experienced in family matters.

   If your care-receiver is mentally competent and able to participate, he or she can be included in your family meetings. You will be talking about his or her life. Imagine how emotionally devastating it would be to have relatives, no matter how loving they might be, make unilateral decisions pertaining to your future without your input.

   Exceptions to including the care-receiver:

   - When you discuss or need to negotiate logistics such as division of caregiving tasks.
   - When family members need to have a united front on a situation, prior to speaking with the care-receiver.
   - When the care-receiver is aggressive or has a belligerent attitude.
   - When the care-receiver suffers from cognitive loss and is unable to make decisions concerning his or her own well-being and future.

2. **Who will lead the meeting?**

   Not all caregivers are comfortable taking on the leadership role in a family meeting. If you have any of the following concerns prior to the meeting, ask someone else to assume it.

   - You would rather concentrate on what you'll be presenting to attendees.
   - You are under a lot of stress and don't want the extra burden of leadership.
   - You feel that certain family members would respond better to a particular individual.
   - You want an ally to be leading the meeting.

   The person chosen to lead the meeting should be someone who is trusted by those attending, does not get easily upset and is known to be fair.

   If past interactions have been contentious and the problems you are now facing are even more sensitive, such as how to pay for care or a nursing home, consider engaging a neutral facilitator. That person could be a social worker, your care-receiver's case manager, if he or she has one, or a religious leader. Be prepared to pay for that service. It may be well worth it.

(Continued on the next page)

A Meeting of the Minds with Family and/or Close-Friends

(Continued)

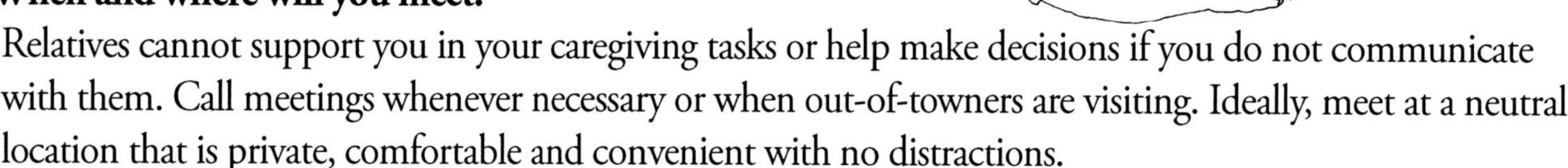

3. When and where will you meet?

Relatives cannot support you in your caregiving tasks or help make decisions if you do not communicate with them. Call meetings whenever necessary or when out-of-towners are visiting. Ideally, meet at a neutral location that is private, comfortable and convenient with no distractions.

You do not need to wait for everyone to be physically present. Thanks to modern technology, family meetings can bring out-of-town relatives together by voice and video phone calls via the Internet or a conference call.

4. What ground rules will govern the meeting?

As in any support group, it is important to set some ground rules. Family members bring a lot of baggage to any gathering. Siblings may still be stuck in old roles: the good or smart child, the bad child or scapegoat, the peacemaker, the lost one, the comedian, etc. They may harbor old grudges or be feuding over real or imagined inequities in the way they perceive they were treated. There may be a certain amount of stress that exists even before the group gets together. The stress may increase when your group discusses urgent and emotional topics such as how to pay for care. Ground rules will help keep the peace.

Examples of ground rules:

We, the family of ____,
will put the well-being of our care-receiver first, before any individual's personal agenda.

We agree to . . .

- avoid bringing up issues from the past.
- discuss only one issue at a time.
- compromise if and when necessary.
- work toward a consensus.
- be aware that everyone present is trying to be helpful.
- treat each other with respect.
- allow everyone to speak, state opinions and express emotions.
- speak only after the other person is finished.
- allow everyone the right to personal opinions, even if everyone is not in agreement.
- mirror back what we think others have said. "Am I correct that you.....?"
- ask for further clarification when necessary.
- express objections in neutral terms.
- avoid blaming, criticizing, making accusations, or saying, "You make me______."
- speak for ourselves only, using "I" sentences. "I think . . . " or "I feel . . ."

Finally, we agree to participate in caring for ________________________, offering physical, emotional, and financial support as needed and possible.

(Continued on the next page)

A Meeting of the Minds with Family and/or Close-Friends

(Continued)

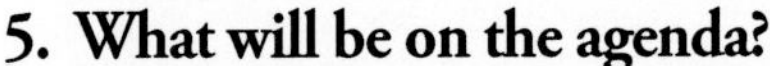

5. What will be on the agenda?

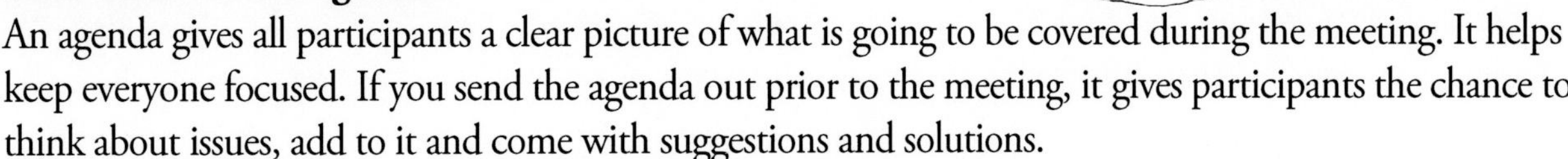

An agenda gives all participants a clear picture of what is going to be covered during the meeting. It helps keep everyone focused. If you send the agenda out prior to the meeting, it gives participants the chance to think about issues, add to it and come with suggestions and solutions.

SAMPLE AGENDA

_______________________ Family and/or Close-Friend Meeting _______________________

CARE-RECEIVER'S NAME DATE, TIME AND PLACE

1. Minutes of last meeting.
2. Latest report from physician. *(Use notes you took during appointment.)*
3. Caregiver's report

   (Use applicable worksheets in this book to help you be focused and factual in your presentation.)
4. What does your care-receiver need and want? If your care-receiver is at the meeting, ask him or her.

   (Include the need for social, emotional, and spiritual connection, as well as mental stimulation.)
5. How can those things be provided? Who is willing to do what?
6. What are the costs? What resources are available?
7. What are your needs as the caregiver?
   (Be honest and specific. This can include help with specific chores, emotional support, the need for respite time and/or vacation time.)
8. How can these needs be addressed?
9. Closing:
   Review the items that have been discussed.
   Review decisions that have been made at this meeting.
   Create a list of the tasks that individuals have agreed to assume, and when.
   Set a date, place and time for next meeting or for an update via e-mail or phone.
10. After the meeting, send a copy of the minutes to all interested parties.

(Continued on the next page)

A Meeting of the Minds with Family and/or Close-Friends

(Continued)

6. Come to the meeting prepared!
The success of the Family and/or Close-Friends meeting depends in a large part on how you, the caregiver, approach it. Treat this family meeting as if it were a friendly business meeting.

A. Know what you want to say, and have examples to substantiate your points.
Bring notes from the care-receiver's last physician's appointment (assessment, new medications, treatment recommendation) and from *Record Keeping Chapter* beginning with page 143.

B. Explain care-receiver's present condition and needs factually and clearly.
Avoid getting defensive when others ask questions. They don't know the situation like you do.
Bring copies from your personal documentation.
Identifying the Level of Assistance Needed, (pages 113–115).

C. State your needs as caregiver factually and clearly.
Be upfront about any physical or medical issues you are dealing with.
Be upfront about your emotional state.
Have a list of tasks that others can do that would make a difference.
Be specific about your need for respite care.

D. Have your calendar with you. Ask family members to mark the days and times they will perform the tasks they've said they would do (shop for groceries, read to the care-receiver, do yard work or laundry, or make a weekly phone call).

7. Expect some conflict – and work through it.
If you have five relatives of a care-receiver in the same room you will probably get at least four different opinions about what needs to be done, especially if it has to do with choices regarding medical care.

Here are some tips that will help the group to keep moving forward …

- When conflicts arise, ask participants to step back for a moment and remember why you are having the meeting in the first place. The welfare of someone important to all of you is at stake.
- Go back to the Ground Rules. If all participants follow them, disagreements can be worked through.
- Weigh both (or all) sides of an issue.
Write down pros and cons of a particular course of action.
Give individuals a chance to explain their position.
Brainstorm for other possible solutions.
- Accept the group decision and request that the group develop a Plan B. That way, should something unexpected occur, you have a fallback position.
- Don't expect that you'll solve all the problems in one meeting. This is an ongoing process.
- Do not insist that caregiving tasks be divided equally. Strive for fairness and solutions. Take into account each person's work and family situation, how close he or she lives to the care-receiver, and each person's resources, skills and interests. The person who can't be there regularly because of work or distance may be willing to stay with your care-receiver while you take a vacation.
- Ask for a time when the task will be completed.
- Express gratitude to everyone for coming to the meeting and offering to help.

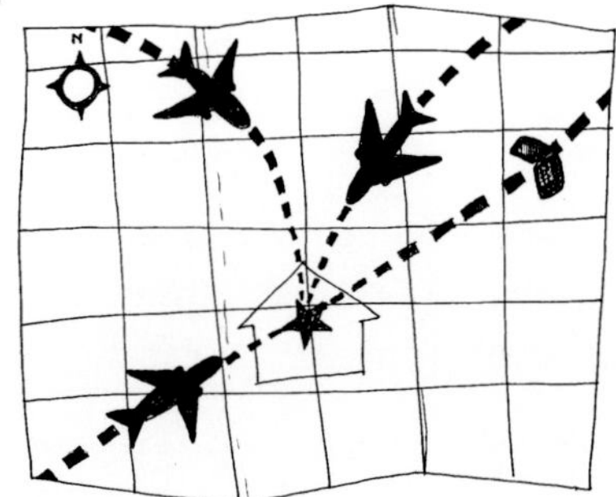

Involving Family and Close Friends

Caregiving is a family and/or a close-friend affair, where everyone needs to work together to help the care-receiver have the best quality of life possible, whether living at home, with a relative or friend, or residing in a care facility of some kind. But in today's mobile society, family and close friends do not always live in the same town or even in the same geographical area; however, they can still provide help.

The value of communication

It would be ideal if family members knew, without being told, what they could do to assist both the care-receiver and the primary caregiver. Unfortunately, that is rarely the way it works. It is usually up to the primary caregiver to let others know the situation and the needs.

Although calling or e-mailing relatives and/or friends individually is helpful, it cannot take the place of family meetings. These personalized meetings allow concerned individuals to discuss the care-receiver's circumstances, make a list of to-do items, and decide who will do them and when.

Everyone can help – in ways that work for them

It is difficult to divide responsibilities evenly when it comes to caregiving, because each person's life situation is different. A relative is more likely to follow through with a task that is compatible with their interests and strengths, work and family commitments, financial situation, and how often they will be able to travel to visit the care-receiver.

Ways that family members other than the primary caregiver can assume:

- Help care-receiver organize important papers *(personal, health, financial, legal, current will, etc.).*
- If needed, manage finances, either online or in person. Set up automatic bill pay. With care-receiver's permission get agreement from utilities to contact you if bills are not paid on time.
- If needed, help caregiver and care-receiver understand and resolve disputes over paperwork *(hospital, healthcare insurance, physician and insurance bills).*
- Research important issues *(nursing home, home healthcare)*.
- Arrange for transportation, household help, home healthcare aide.
- Check references of potential healthcare professionals or aides.
- Arrange and/or help pay for respite care, or schedule a visit and provide respite care personally.
- Do household repairs, yard work.
- Spend quality time with care-receiver, offering emotional support, sharing memories, etc. Encourage him or her to express feelings, talk about what he or she wants and what's most important at this time.
- Communicate on the telephone or internet, send cards, e-mails, letters, small "I love you" gifts.
- With your care-receiver's written consent, establish a relationship with each of his or her doctors and keep an updated list of medications.

Other ideas:

1. ______________________________
2. ______________________________
3. ______________________________

Action Plan for a Long-Distance Caregiver

If you do not live near a close relative or friend who needs help, yet you are the one he or she relies on, you are a long-distance caregiver. This Action Plan will help you respond to situations as effectively as possible from where you live. Use the reverse side of this paper if you need more room to write. Consider putting all the information in your caregiver's notebook.

1. **Compile contact information relating to the care of your relative (not all may be applicable). Include name, contact information and best time to call:**

   Physicians ______________________________

   ____

   Attorney ______________________________
   Financial advisor and/or manager______________________________
   Healthcare aide and or agency ______________________________
   Church outreach (if care-receiver is affiliated with a denomination) ______________________________

2. **If you do not have power of attorney for your care-receiver, obtain signed consent forms allowing you to communicate with care-receiver's physicians, financial advisor, etc.**

   Have you filled out the forms on pages ______________?

3. **Be in contact with each of your care-receiver's doctors and be aware of all medications.**

   Who is each doctor's nurse? ______________________________

4. **If the care-receiver is in an assisted living or nursing facility, know his or her case manager, facility manager and nurses, and each one's contact information. Include friends, too.**

   *Who are these individuals?*______________________________

   ____

5. **If your care-receiver is living at home but has no local primary caregiver, consider engaging a professional who can act as his or her advocate or case manager. Local government agencies may be able to direct you in this effort.**

   What agency will you contact? ______________________________
   *Phone number?*______________ *e-mail?* ______________________________

6. **Speak regularly to the in-town caregiver, a relative or a close neighbor who can report on the care-receiver's situation. If the care-receiver is in a facility, talk to his or her case manager.**

   Who will you call? ______________________________

7. **Consider helping care-receiver set up automatic bill payment wherever possible.**

   *What monthly bills could be put on this system?*______________________________

8. **Line up resources your care-receiver might use.**

   Grocery stores that deliver – include online options
   Senior transportation – look for a non-profit organization providing no- or low-cost service.
   Housekeeper – be sure to get references.
   Handyman – look for an organization that sends volunteers to do chores.

Identifying the Level of Assistance Needed

The purpose of this worksheet is to offer you concrete examples to share at a family meeting focusing on identifying the level of assistance your care-receiver needs.

How able is ______________________________ **to perform the following functions?**
YOUR CARE-RECEIVER

Housework: ❑ Needs No Help ❑ Minimal Help ❑ Lots of Help ❑ Complete Help

- Specifics I have noticed ______________________________
- How family and/or close friends can help ______________________________
- Other solutions ______________________________
- Action Plan ______________________________

Taking medications as prescribed: ❑ Needs No Help ❑ Minimal Help ❑ Lots of Help ❑ Complete Help

- Specifics I have noticed ______________________________
- How family and/or close friends can help ______________________________
- Other solutions ______________________________
- Action Plan ______________________________

Managing finances: ❑ Needs No Help ❑ Minimal Help ❑ Lots of Help ❑ Complete Help

- Specifics I have noticed ______________________________
- How family and/or close friends can help ______________________________
- Other solutions ______________________________
- Action Plan ______________________________

Shopping: ❑ Needs No Help ❑ Minimal Help ❑ Lots of Help ❑ Complete Help

- Specifics I have noticed ______________________________
- How family and/or close friends can help ______________________________
- Other solutions ______________________________
- Action Plan ______________________________

(Continued on the next page)

Identifying the Level of Assistance Needed *(Continued)*

The purpose of this worksheet is to offer you concrete examples to share at a family meeting focusing on identifying the level of assistance your care-receiver needs.

How able is ______________________________ **to perform the following functions?**
YOUR CARE-RECEIVER

Use of phone and other communications: ❑ Needs No Help ❑ Minimal Help ❑ Lots of Help ❑ Complete Help

- Specifics I have noticed ______________________________
- How family and/or close friends can help ______________________________
- Other solutions ______________________________
- Action Plan ______________________________

Use of technology and other equipment: ❑ Needs No Help ❑ Minimal Help ❑ Lots of Help ❑ Complete Help

- Specifics I have noticed ______________________________
- How family and/or close friends can help ______________________________
- Other solutions ______________________________
- Action Plan ______________________________

Transportation, can drive or arrange: ❑ Needs No Help ❑ Minimal Help ❑ Lots of Help ❑ Complete Help

- Specifics I have noticed ______________________________
- How family and/or close friends can help ______________________________
- Other solutions ______________________________
- Action Plan ______________________________

Other: ❑ Needs No Help ❑ Minimal Help ❑ Lots of Help ❑ Complete Help

- Specifics I have noticed ______________________________
- How family and/or close friends can help ______________________________
- Other solutions ______________________________
- Action Plan ______________________________

(Continued on the next page)

Identifying the Level of Assistance Needed *(Continued)*

How well can ______________________________ **perform the following functions without help?**
CARE-RECEIVER'S NAME

1. Personal hygiene and grooming

	YES	NO	SOMETIMES
Can your care-receiver get in and out of tub or shower without help?			
Can your care-receiver bathe self (except for back)?			
Can your care-receiver clean genital area after using the toilet?			
Does your care-receiver remember to do these things?			

Specifics I have noticed ______________________________

2. Dressing and undressing

	YES	NO	SOMETIMES
Can your care-receiver get clothing from dresser or closet, put items on and fasten correctly without help?			
Does your care-receiver need to be dressed?			

Specifics I have noticed ______________________________

3. Toileting

	YES	NO	SOMETIMES
Can your care-receiver get on and off toilet, clean private area, zip up or pull up pants or pull down dress without assistance?			

Specifics I have noticed ______________________________

4. Continence

	YES	NO	SOMETIMES
Does your care-receiver have control of bowel and bladder?			

Specifics I have noticed ______________________________

5. Transferring

	YES	NO	SOMETIMES
Can your care-receiver get in and out of bed without help?			
Can your care-receiver get in and out of chairs without assistance?			

Specifics I have noticed ______________________________

6. Feeding

	YES	NO	SOMETIMES
Can your care-receiver get food from the plate into his or her mouth without help?			
Can your care-receiver drink from a glass or straw without help?			

Specifics I have noticed ______________________________

7. Ambulation

	YES	NO	SOMETIMES
Can your care-receiver walk, using an assistive device if needed?			
Does your care-receiver use a wheelchair?			

Specifics I have noticed ______________________________

Visitors are Coming!

Isolation is one of the main difficulties faced by caregivers and care-receivers. Having others come to visit can be a pleasant break in that isolation. In order for it to be satisfying, you as a caregiver will need to do some planning. Inform visitors of the nature of the illness, special circumstances that may make communication difficult, and topics of conversation that it might be well to avoid. By explaining these and other concerns to visitors ahead of time, you smooth the way for a pleasant time for all concerned.

Also, give your care-receiver plenty of notice of the visit to ensure his or her being prepared.

Tips for making visits pleasant:

1. Reach out to others. Often family and friends are not sure if a visit would be welcome. Let them know that you and your care-receiver would appreciate spending time with them. Then go one step further and suggest a day and time, keeping in mind the time of day when you and your care-receiver are at your best.

2. Let your visitors know what to expect. Sometimes visitors underestimate the ways an illness has affected the care-receiver. Other times, they may over-dramatize the situation. That is why it is so important to explain your care-receiver's condition, the ways in which he or she has changed, and how best to communicate with him or her. This is especially important when there is some level of dementia. If visitors have come to the home previously, explain any changes that may have occurred since then. If they know what to expect they will be more at ease.

3. Have suggestions ready if visitors ask what they can bring. Make a list of the things your care-receiver enjoys, keeping in mind any changes in ability to focus, understand, or do things with his or her hands. Your list might include books, magazines, puzzles, books on tape, a movie DVD, a treat such as ice cream or chocolate, flowers, and photos of family members or of events the visitors and the care-receiver attended together. The latter can open the door to talking about happy memories.

4. Also suggest activities they might do with your care-receiver. Working on a puzzle together or playing a game can be a pleasant way of spending time together. Or, if the visitors are willing and your care-receiver is up to it, suggest they take him or her on a short outing. For example, they might go to lunch, visit a park or walk around the block.

5. Encourage young visitors to share their interests. Children might enjoy playing their recital piece on the piano, explaining something they are learning in school, or perhaps bringing a pet. Looking at photos of family and asking questions about the past can bring the generations closer together.

6. Remember your visitors are not expecting you to fuss. Remind yourself that you do not need to prepare for visitors the way you used to. No need to give the house a thorough cleaning and make a snack or meal. Friends and relatives will not expect that of you. They will appreciate your being present or nearby, in case they need help understanding or assisting the care-receiver.

7. Accept offers of help, but do not expect them to take over while you leave. Visitors want to be helpful. If they ask what they can do while at your home, think of a small task you have been wanting to accomplish. However, not everyone will be comfortable with being left alone with your care-receiver while you run an errand or take a walk. If that is what you need most, discuss it with them first.

8. Make sure your visitors know that their presence is the greatest gift. Stop what you are doing and spend at least a little time with family and friends who come to visit. Express your gratitude for their visit.

SHARE YOUR OWN TIPS WITH OTHERS IN THE ROOM.

Practical Holiday Tips

Shifting your attitude can help you enjoy the holidays.

Be realistic – don't compare this holiday to the "good ole days"

- Create new traditions that are appropriate for right now.
- Minimize decorations, gifts, and clutter.
- Give gifts that require minimum shopping time. Send checks or gift cards, order from catalogues or shop the Internet.
- Avoid over-spending. Sticking to your budget will minimize after-the-holidays stress.
- Schedule events early in the day when you and your care-receiver have the most energy.

Let others know what you need

- If people ask what gifts you'd like, share a wish list: visits and/or regular phone calls to the caregiver, handyman around the house, shopping and other tasks.
- If you have company, allow (and expect) them to help you. Line up help. Say YES to offers of help, meals, company and gifts of kindness and love.
- Acknowledge your feelings. You don't need to feel *happy* even if it is a holiday.
- Say NO. People will understand if you can't participate in the usual parties.

Take care of yourself

- Avoid over-indulgence in food and drink.
- Keep to your regular schedule. It is helpful for both you and your care-receiver.
- Find time to exercise even though you're busy.
- Get enough sleep – or as much as possible.
- Don't overdo.
- Make time for yourself - when or where you have no distractions.
- Seek professional help if you are unusually sad or anxious.
- Attend a religious, spiritual, or community event, if possible.

Focus on good family relationships

- Avoid family disagreements.
- Set aside family differences – accept family as they are.
- Connect with family by phone, e-mail or cards.

Getting a Handle on Holiday Blues

It is common for both caregivers and care-receivers to experience holiday blues – feelings of sadness, loneliness, depression and anxiety, while other people seem to be celebrating.

Complete the following statements.

How will this______________________________be different from the past?
(HOLIDAY)

How can you adapt and create new traditions? ____________________

For what are you grateful on this holiday? ____________________

How can you connect with close friends and family on this holiday? ____________________

How can you connect with those in a similar situation on this holiday? ____________________

How can you connect with your religion and/or spirituality on this holiday? ____________________

If you have company, how can they help your care-receiver? ____________________

If you have company, how can they help you? ____________________

How can you make this a special time for your care-receiver? ____________________

How can you make this a special time for yourself? ____________________

Any tips you can share? ____________________

Talking about End-of-Life Issues

Caregivers whose care-receiver has a progressively debilitating disease or a negative prognosis will inevitably find themselves faced with the need to discuss end-of-life topics, which include the following:

- whether or not to begin hospice-care.
- the type of care that he or she would want if hospitalized and unable to communicate *(extreme measures).*
- the disposition of care-receiver's worldly goods.
- care-receiver's last wishes *(visiting with memorable people or clergy, doing something special).*
- how the care-receiver would like his or her life to be honored *(funeral, celebration of life).*

Sometimes caregiver, care-receiver and family members may hesitate to bring up these topics, but doing so can benefit all involved. Once the unspoken is out in the open, appropriate plans can be made. The care-receiver's feelings of loneliness, isolation and fear of the unknown can be replaced by the comfort of being assured that someone will see that his or her wishes are honored. This makes it possible for the caregiver, care-receiver and others to spend the time that remains, saying what they need to say to each other and moving toward acceptance of the inevitable.

Remember, your job as caregiver is to *assist* your care-receiver in planning for this important stage of life. When talking to him or her, let your attitude be one of acceptance and support, even if his or her choices in these areas do not agree with your own. However, you may need to take a more assertive approach if he or she has not yet put legal documents in place, such as a Final Will and Testament, Durable Power of Health Care and Financial Power of Attorney, Living Will or Advance Directive.

As a Caregiver, You're on the Front Line

If your care-receiver doesn't have these crucial documents on file, encourage him or her to make an appointment with an eldercare lawyer as soon as possible. This is especially true of an Advance Directive or Living Will. If a medical crisis or dementia render the care-receiver unable to make decisions regarding his or her care, you and/ or family members could be left to do so without a clear understanding of his or her wishes. That can, and often does, lead to family conflict.

As the person most intimately involved with the care-receiver, you are likely to be the one he or she has spoken to about wishes for end-of-life medical care. Also, *you are the one most likely to get the brunt of the family's anger if they do not understand or agree with what you know to be the care-receiver's wishes, especially if you cannot prove she or he communicated them to you.*

Thus it is important that you and your care-receiver talk about all the end-of-life issues mentioned above. Share the information about last wishes and how the care-receiver wants his or her life to be honored, preferably in written form. Assist your care-receiver in having a document drawn up that gives you (or another trusted person) the legal standing to make sure end-of-life medical care wishes are communicated and carried out.

It is crucial that open, supportive communication be established before tackling these difficult issues. Reviewing the suggestions in the section *Touchy Topics, Sensitive Conversations,* page 101, and answering the questions on the next page, 120, *Am I Ready to have this Conversation*, can help you prepare yourself for this discussion.

(Continued on the next page)

Talking about End-of-Life Issues *(Continued)*

Am I ready to have this conversation?

Y N

❑ ❑ 1. I am clear about my reasons for bringing up the topic.

❑ ❑ 2. I am in a good place emotionally.

❑ ❑ 3. I have given a great deal of thought to how best to approach the subject.

❑ ❑ 4. I am willing to let my care-receiver take the time she or he needs to think through the issues.

❑ ❑ 5. I am able to be an empathetic listener.

❑ ❑ 6. I am prepared to deal with care-receiver's fear, anger, regret or other realistic emotions that may surface.

❑ ❑ 7. I am willing to accept my care-receiver's desires for himself or herself without pushing my own thoughts and beliefs.

❑ ❑ 8. I am able to be silent, if that is appropriate.

❑ ❑ 9. I'm not angry or upset with my care-receiver.

Is your care-receiver ready to have the conversation?

Y N

❑ ❑ 1. Is your care-receiver in pain?

❑ ❑ 2. Is your care-receiver rested?

❑ ❑ 3. Has your care-receiver indicated a concern or willingness to talk about end-of-life issues?

❑ ❑ 4. Is your care-receiver experiencing fear, anger, regret or other negative and/or realistic emotions he or she wishes to talk about?

❑ ❑ 5. Is your care-receiver able to understand the issues and express his or her desires?

What do I want? A care-receiver's worksheet

If your care-receiver has difficulty thinking or talking about emotional issues, the worksheet, *What do I want?* page 121, may be helpful. It can be used to elicit information on a variety of topics, ranging from what the care-receiver wants from home healthcare to the kind of funeral service or celebration of life he or she wishes.

The point of these conversations is to allow the care-receiver free expression of what is important. You might not like or agree with the response to these questions, but you need to listen to and attempt to honor what is said.

(Continued on the next page)

What Do I Want?

Ask your care-receiver to complete this page, either in writing or verbally. This may take some time.

I am thinking about ____

____

____

Here are three things (or more) that I know for sure that I DO want.

____

____

____

Here are three things (or more) that I know for sure that I DO NOT want.

____

____

____

Here are three things (or more) that I am not sure about and am still contemplating.

____

____

____

My biggest fear is ____

____

____

What single thing, if addressed by your care-receiver, family and closest friends, would offer you the most comfort?

____

____

____

Being an Advocate for your Care-Receiver

CHAPTER 6

In most cases, primary caregivers become the healthcare advocate for their care-receivers. This chapter provides information on what is necessary for effective advocacy, including doctor's visits, crisis preparation and home safety.

A Circle of Unending Love and Compassion

Life is a circle
of giving love
and being loved,
of giving care
and receiving care,
a circle of unending compassion.

To give is to receive.
As you sow,
so shall you reap.

In giving to others,
you shall receive tenfold.
To give is to receive.

Life is a circle, a circle of unending love.

by Sherokee Ilse

The Caregiver as a Healthcare Advocate

It is difficult for care-receivers to navigate the medical system and coordinate their own care. Helping them to do so is probably one of the most important tasks caregivers perform in their role as advocate for their care-receiver. This includes understanding the impact and progression of the condition on the care-receiver's abilities, making medical appointments, accompanying the care-receiver to those appointments, making sure he or she takes medication as prescribed, following up on other physician instructions, and finding alternatives if they are not satisfied with the care they are receiving.

This calls for …

- knowledge
- patience
- determination
- organization
- follow-up
- assertion without aggression
- being another ear – someone who knows what the doctor, nurse, etc., has said

It is important to …

- have a conversation with the care-receiver in which both of you are clear about the kind of support that is wanted and/or needed. This may need to happen from time-to-time.
- help care-receiver prepare for the appointment.
- take notes at all appointments and conversations.
- give your perspective on how your care-receiver is doing; keep comments to the point.
- ask questions and make comments when appropriate.
- advocate for your care-receiver if he or she is hospitalized (request warm blanket, take doctor and/or nurse outside of the room in a private place for serious conversations).
- allow care-receiver to do most the talking; direct the doctor or nurse to speak to him or her.

If and when you are the person in charge …

- have all medical records handy.
- have a signed consent form on file with all of your care-receiver's physicians, allowing you to communicate directly.
- obtain an advance healthcare directive (Living Will, Advance Healthcare Directive, The Five Wishes, etc.) This legal document specifies the medical actions an individual authorizes in the event he or she is unable to make decisions regarding his or her care. It can be very important during a visit to the emergency room or an overnight hospitalization. It has much more power than your verbal statement of your care-receiver's wishes.
- obtain a healthcare power of attorney.
- take the time to talk to your care-receiver about end-of-life wishes (see page 119–120).
- consult your attorney about the next steps.
- obtain basic forms from your local senior center or the Internet.
- have forms notarized after completion.
- have signed legal documents authorizing you and a designated back-up person to make decisions on your care-receiver's behalf if incapacitated. This legal document may be called *power of healthcare attorney, medical power of attorney or healthcare proxy.*

(Continued on the next page)

The Caregiver as a Healthcare Advocate *(Continued)*

Educate yourself

- Learn all you can about your care-receiver's condition. Become familiar with the symptoms, what you can expect at the various stages and the treatments available. Pamphlets are usually at your care-receiver's physician's office.
- Ask questions during doctor's appointments. Take careful notes.
- Use the Internet to check reliable medical websites associated with established medical institutions.
- Find information on the sites of disease-specific national organizations.
- Attend a caregiver support group affiliated with an organization dedicated to the specific issue.

Organize important papers

If you have not already done so, follow the suggestions given in the Record Keeping section. It will take time to set up the various tracking pages, however it will ultimately save you time and minimize stress. Use the forms or your version of them to help you keep information at your fingertips. Even if you prefer to document on the computer, have printed copies handy.

1. *Caregiver's Log* – page 146
2. *Substitute Caregiver's Information* – pages 147–153
3. *Financial Records* – page 154
4. *Care-Receiver's Personal Records* – page 131–132

Get the most out of doctor's appointments

Care-receivers often do not understand and/or remember what was said during a doctor's appointment. As the advocate, make sure important information is understood and followed.

I . Prepare

A. Ask your care-receiver for information the doctor should know. For example, is he or she experiencing pain or new symptoms?

B. Are there sensitive subjects that your care-receiver would prefer that you speak about with the physician, such as incontinence or depression?

C. Use your *Caregiver's Log*, page 146, to remind you of problems and/or new symptoms you have noted in the time since the last visit. If there are new symptoms, note when they started, what was happening and where you were at the time. Also note anything the care-receiver is doing or taking to mitigate the problem.

D. Make a list of everything you and your care-receiver want to discuss, in order of priority. There may not be time to discuss everything on the list, so you want to be sure the most important topics are covered first.

E. Bring a list of all medications your care-receiver is taking, including those prescribed by other physicians, over-the-counter pills, vitamins, and/or homeopathic or natural remedies. Refer to *Medications*, page 158.

F. Have the care-receiver's primary, secondary and/or prescription insurance cards ready.

G. If the physician does not have a copy of the care-receiver's advance directives, bring one with you to the appointment.

H. Keep empty pages in your notebook for notes on any treatments or changes in routine recommended by your care-receiver's doctors.

(Continued on the next page)

The Caregiver as a Healthcare Advocate

Get the most out of doctors' appointments *(Continued)*

II. The appointment

- If possible, make the appointment for the time of day when your care-receiver is at his or her best.
- Remind him or her the day before and the morning of the appointment.
- Give yourself plenty of time to get ready.
- Stay calm if you have to wait for the doctor even though you have arrived on time. (You might want to call the doctor's office to see if he or she is running on time before you leave home.)
- Bring magazines, books, cross-word puzzle books, music or audio books on iPod (especially for blind care-receivers), for both of you.

III. Clear communication

- Know the office administrator, receptionist and/or nurses names, extension number, fax number and/or e-mail. Call them by their name.
- Care-receivers need to feel they have a say in regard to their medical treatment. Allow your care-receiver to speak for himself or herself, stating how he or she sees the situation and answer the doctor's questions. Add information that you think is important for the doctor to know.
- If the doctor or nurse practitioner talks directly to you instead of the care-receiver, redirect them toward the care-receiver.
- Do not hesitate to ask for more information about tests the physician wants to order.
- Be sure you are completely clear about any instructions, i.e., fasting, drinking water, etc. Take careful notes.
- If there is a change in medication, ask the reason, if the new medication is covered by insurance, and whether there is a less expensive, generic form available.
- Do not count on remembering everything said at the appointment. Take notes. Consider recording doctor's visits, especially when a diagnosis and/or treatment are being discussed. Use these notes or recordings when discussing with family members later.
- It is most helpful if you and your care-receiver are open and honest about everything that is happening. Share your feelings. Tell your doctor if either one of you are dissatisfied with how things are going.
- Ask for referrals if you think a second opinion would be useful.
- Ask if you may communicate with the physician by e-mail.

(Continued on the next page)

The Caregiver as a Healthcare Advocate

Get the most out of doctor appointments *(Continued)*

IV. Ready for a trip to emergency room?

A trip to the emergency room is always stressful, but can be less so if you are prepared.

A. Create an emergency card for your care-receiver's purse or wallet
In case your care-receiver will need emergency help when you are not present, prepare an emergency list with the following information: name, date of birth, physicians' names and numbers, medical conditions, medications and doses, allergies, plus emergency contact information. Carry a copy of your own.

B. Have an emergency kit ready to go (See *Crisis Preparation*, page 130)

C. When to go to the emergency room
Your care-receiver may need to be taken to the emergency room if any of the following symptoms are present: Shortness of breath, difficulty speaking, severe pain, weakness on one side of the body, severe vomiting or diarrhea, fainting, sudden dizziness, uncontrolled bleeding, changes in vision.

D. Know the fastest route to the hospital of preference.
If you are driving, be sure to know the best way, plus an alternate route.

E. Call an ambulance when …

- your care-receiver's condition appears to be life-threatening.
- your attempt to move your care-receiver might make the situation worse.
- traffic or weather conditions could be a delay.
- you are in doubt.

V. When your care-receiver has been hospitalized …

- Make sure your contact number is on your care-receiver's chart. If someone else has been designated as healthcare proxy or holds power of attorney, that information should be there also.
- Obtain the name of the attending physician. Ask the best way to contact him or her.
- Learn all you can about your care-receiver's condition. Ask questions about tests that are ordered and the treatment he or she is receiving. Take notes.
- Support your care-receiver in his or her choices regarding treatment. If he or she is not able to make healthcare decisions and you are the designated healthcare power of attorney, use his or her advance healthcare directive as a guide to make sure his or her wishes are followed.
- Keep family members and friends up-to-date regarding your care-receiver's situation. If you have not already done so, find someone willing to pass information on to those on your list, or post updates on a website such as Caring Bridge.
- Talk to a hospital social worker or other appropriate person regarding discharge planning. You will need to know whether your care-receiver will be going home, or to someone else's home, a rehabilitation facility or a nursing home.
- Get to know the staff. Show your appreciation with thanks and treats.

Take care of yourself. Get rest. Call on relatives and friends for help!

Medication Management

Administering medications properly — or helping the care-receiver to take them as prescribed — can be complicated, especially when the care-receiver is taking many different medications, each with its own schedule. Knowing the five "medication rights" will help you administer your care-receiver's medications properly.

Make sure…

the **right person**
receives the **right medication**
in the **right dose**
at the **right time**
via the **right method.**

The following hints can also help you feel confident about monitoring or dispensing medication.

1. **Keep an updated list or chart of all the care-receiver's medications and how they are used** (see page 158). You may want to put a small picture of each medication next to the name to prevent medication mix-ups.
   Put a copy of your list or chart with the care-receiver's other medical records, one in your crisis kit (see page 130), and one in the care-receiver's purse or wallet. Also post one on the refrigerator where emergency personnel would be able see it, in the event you weren't present.

2. **Make sure you understand the reason for each medication**, its proper use and potential side effects. If you have questions, consult your care-receiver's pharmacist or physician. Have the pharmacist check each new prescription to make sure it is compatible with other medications being taken by your care-receiver. Report any side effects to the prescribing physician.

3. **Ask your care-receiver's physician or pharmacist for a periodic medication review**. Take in all medications the care-receiver uses, including over-the-counter meds and/or homeopathic remedies. This will minimize the risk of over-medication and/or harmful drug interactions.

4. **Use a pill container to make dispensing meds in the form of pills easier and more accurate.** These organizers range from simple to automated, weekly to monthly. They typically have removable daily strips with divisions for morning, noon, evening and bedtime. Versions with built-in timers and alarms can be very helpful when pills must be taken every 2 or 3 hours. Lockable dispensers can prevent a person with dementia from double-dosing or taking pills at the wrong time of day.

5. **Save on prescription costs** by ordering a three-month's supply of meds at a time through the mail-order company associated with your care-receiver's drug insurance plan. If you are using a local pharmacy instead, fill all prescriptions at the same place. Many pharmacies automatically check the customer's prescription history for drug interactions when customers bring a new script.

6. **Properly dispose of unused or out-of-date medications.** Fire stations and clinics often have disposal drops.

Knowledge is Power

Knowing the specifics of the condition or disease of your care-receiver will shed light on the struggles he or she faces.

What is the condition or disease called? ______________________________

____

What are his or her typical symptoms? ______________________________

____

____

Where can you get more information about it? ______________________________

____

What are some obstacles your care-receiver faces? ______________________________

____

____

What can you or your care-receiver expect in the next 6 months? ______________________________

____

____

What frustrations does your care-receiver deal with on a daily basis? ______________________________

____

____

How can you, as a caregiver, help your care-receiver do the best he or she can do?

____

____

____

What can you, as a caregiver, do to keep yourself doing the best you can do?

____

____

____

Crisis Preparation

At some point, you may need to accompany your care-receiver to the hospital in an emergency situation. Having everything ready and in a designated spot will reduce the stress of gathering up items you will need.

Important information

- A list of contact telephone numbers and e-mails (family, friends, clergy).
- List of all medications, with a schedule of how they were being taken at home, prior to admission. Take a few copies of each with you.
- ALL physicians' names, specialties, phone and fax numbers. Take a few copies of each with you.
- Names of people you interact with in the offices of your physicians.
- List of previous hospitalizations and surgeries (dates, physician, reason).
- All insurance cards.
- List of special circumstances the people in the hospital should know.
- Copies of living will, advance directive, power of health care attorney, etc.
- Recent health history. Take a few copies of each with you.
- Photo identification card.

You might also wish to take a copy of *Care-Receiver's Personal Records,* pages 131 and 132.

Items to bring for your care-receiver who is being hospitalized

- Night-time items (pajamas, nightgown, bathrobe, non-skid slippers).
- Toiletries (toothbrush, toothpaste and razor).
- Personal items (eyeglasses, dentures, hearing aids, batteries).
- Cash for incidentals (magazines or items from gift shop).
- Electronics (Cell phone, iPad and chargers).
- Comfort items (stuffed animal, photograph of a loved one).

Caregiver's care package

- Your caregiver's log book
- Address book
- Cell phone
- Notebook, marker, pens, pencils
- Invisible tape, sticky notes
- Paper clips, small stapler
- Note cards or stationary, stamps
- Book to read
- Music to listen to
- Sweater or lap robe and small pillow
- Money to buy beverages and food
- Knitting, sketch pad, other interests
- Medications, supplements, etc.

Care-Receiver's Personal Records

Legal Name ______________________________

Address ____________________ City____________ State________ Zip________

Telephone Number ____________________ Cell phone____________________

Social Security Number ______________________________

Birth Certificate Date of Birth ____________ Location ____________________

Name on certificate ____________________ City ____________ State/Country ____________

Father's Name ____________________ Mother's Name ____________________

Marriage License Location ______________________________ Date ____________

Divorce Record Location ______________________________ Date____________

Attorney ______________________________ Phone ____________________

Military Records Location ____________________ Military ID # ____________________

Branch of Military ____________________ Contact Phone ____________________

Military Retirement Benefits ______________________________

Last Will and Testament, Power of Attorney and other Legal Health Documents

Location ____________________ Attorney ____________________ Phone ____________

Insurance Policies Location ______________________________

Insurance Co.	Phone number	Policy Number	Beneficiary	Value

Memorial Plan Name of Funeral Home ______________________________

Contact Person ______________________________ Phone ____________________

Cemetery Name ______________________________

Contact Person ______________________________ Phone ____________________

(Continued on the next page)

Care Receiver's Personal Records *(Continued)*

Safety Deposit Box Location ______________________ Key Location______________________

Who is authorized to open? ______________________ Contents ______________________

Retirement Information ______________________

Contact ______________________ Phone ______________________

Contact ______________________ Phone ______________________

Contact ______________________ Phone ______________________

Investments Information ______________________

Contact ______________________ Phone ______________________

Contact ______________________ Phone ______________________

Contact ______________________ Phone ______________________

Deed to Property Location ______________________

Mortgage Co. ______________Contact ______________ Phone ______________

Mortgage Co. ______________Contact ______________ Phone ______________

Mortgage Co. ______________Contact ______________ Phone ______________

Vehicle Ownership Title Location ______________________

Loan Co. __________ ID# __________ Year ________ Make ________ Model ________

Loan Co. __________ ID# __________ Year ________ Make ________ Model ________

Loan Co. __________ ID# __________ Year ________ Make ________ Model ________

Debit or Credit Card Location ______________________

Card Company	Name on Account	Account Number	Contact Phone

Loans

Type of Loan	Loaner – Person/Co.	Document Location	Contact Phone

Tax Records Location ______________________

Accountant's Name ______________________ Phone ______________________

Am I "Helping" Too Much?

With the desire to do what is best for the care-receiver, caregivers can, and sometimes do, step over the fine line between

- actions that are helpful and/or necessary to the care-receiver, and
- actions that, though well-meaning, demean the care-receiver and/or deprive them of choice and their sense of personhood.

It is not always easy to sense the difference between taking a necessary action and carrying it to an extreme that is not healthy for you or your care receiver. Often caregivers do not realize they are encroaching on that line until their actions begin to cause problems. That can be avoided by periodically asking your care-receiver if you are helping in ways that makes him or her feel cared for and acknowledged as a person.

Be prepared to accept his or her perception of your caring. If he or she objects to some of your actions or attitudes, ask what you might change that would make a difference. Work together to find a satisfying solution. Even if your care-receiver is not able to articulate clearly what actions are disturbing, paying attention to his or her body language and emotions can tell you a great deal.

As you go through the examples below, consider if your way of helping is closer to the smiling example or the frowning example.

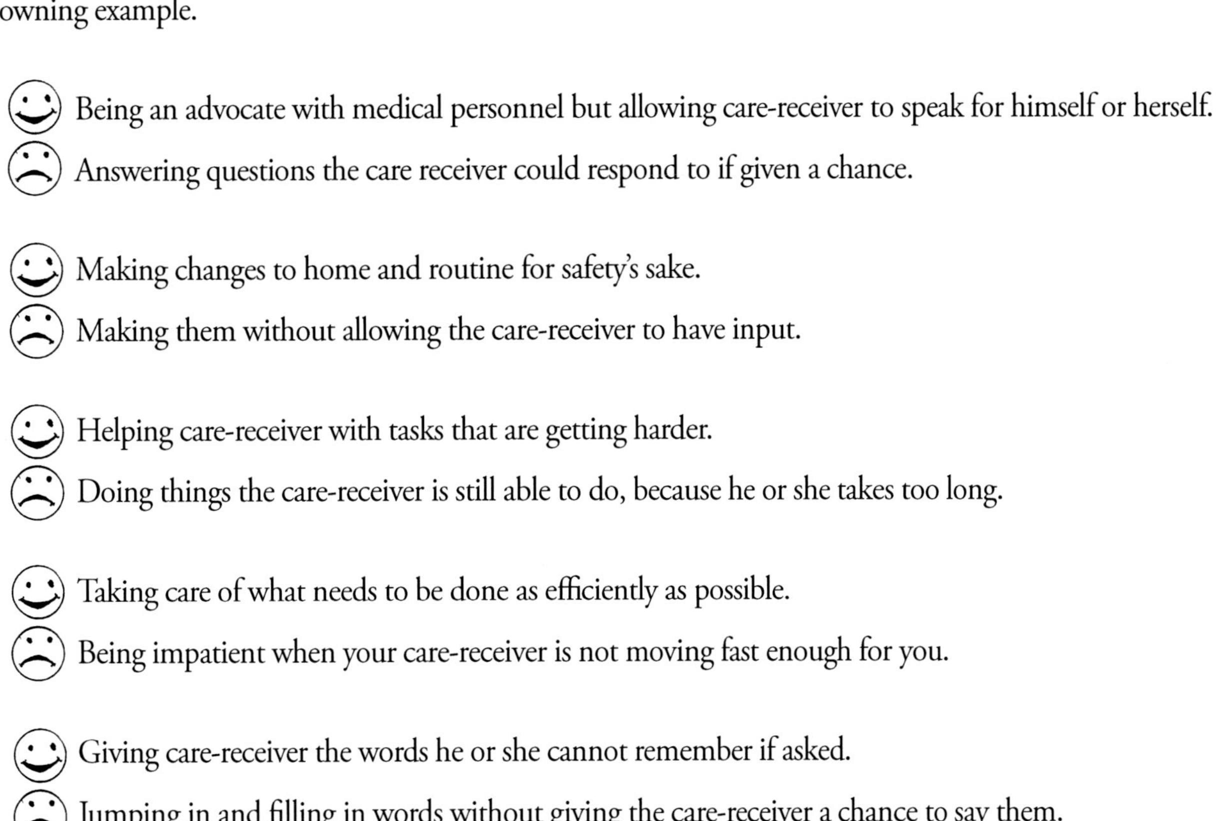

Being an advocate with medical personnel but allowing care-receiver to speak for himself or herself.

Answering questions the care receiver could respond to if given a chance.

Making changes to home and routine for safety's sake.

Making them without allowing the care-receiver to have input.

Helping care-receiver with tasks that are getting harder.

Doing things the care-receiver is still able to do, because he or she takes too long.

Taking care of what needs to be done as efficiently as possible.

Being impatient when your care-receiver is not moving fast enough for you.

Giving care-receiver the words he or she cannot remember if asked.

Jumping in and filling in words without giving the care-receiver a chance to say them.

Making everyday household decisions together.

Making decision without asking for input.

Is Your Care-Receiver's Home Safe?

Check with your fire department regarding a free safety evaluation.

	YES	NO
OUTSIDE ENTRANCES		
Outdoor lights by home entrances and garage	❑	❑
Secure railing	❑	❑
Peephole in front door	❑	❑
Working lock	❑	❑
Lock box with extra key	❑	❑
ELECTRIC		
Bright lighting to eliminate shadows	❑	❑
Nightlights in many places	❑	❑
Switches, easy to turn on and off	❑	❑
Multiple switches marked	❑	❑
Outlets grounded	❑	❑
Smoke detectors where appropriate	❑	❑
Alarm system	❑	❑
Loud doorbell	❑	❑
Extension cords in perfect shape	❑	❑
GARAGE		
Clean	❑	❑
Clear passageways	❑	❑
DRIVEWAY		
Clear and easy passageway	❑	❑
No broken pavement	❑	❑
WINDOWS and DOORS		
Easy to open and close	❑	❑
Doorways wide enough to maneuver	❑	❑
Front door view panel or peephole	❑	❑
Locks easy to use	❑	❑
Windows and doors easy to open and close	❑	❑
OUTSIDE		
Ramp, if needed	❑	❑
Lights along entrance	❑	❑
Handrails on steps	❑	❑
Sand or salt on ice	❑	❑
Steps, driveway, walkways, porch, decks, patios clear	❑	❑
No spills, puddles, ice, snow	❑	❑
Walkways clear of debris	❑	❑
No uneven or cracked walkways	❑	❑

(Continued on the next page)

Is Your Care-Receiver's Home Safe? *(Continued)*

	YES	NO
TELEPHONES		
Enough telephones	❑	❑
One home or cell telephone within reach at all times	❑	❑
Telephones with volume control and large numbers	❑	❑
Emergency phone numbers posted by all phones	❑	❑
Speed dial set to 911 on all cell and home phones	❑	❑
IN GENERAL INSIDE THE HOME		
Adequate smoke detectors	❑	❑
Carbon monoxide detector	❑	❑
Electrical cords in perfect shape	❑	❑
No hot-to-touch outlets or switches	❑	❑
Enough bright lighting everywhere	❑	❑
Pest-free	❑	❑
Plumbing and utilities all in working order	❑	❑
Mail easy to retrieve	❑	❑
Medicines in original containers and marked	❑	❑
Pathways clear of clutter and electric cords	❑	❑
No throw rugs	❑	❑
Furniture arranged so no clutter or obstacles	❑	❑
Hot water heater not set too high	❑	❑
FLOORS		
Safe surfaces, not waxed	❑	❑
Throw rugs removed	❑	❑
Carpeting in good shape	❑	❑
Changes in floor levels clearly marked with reflective tape	❑	❑
STAIRS		
Good lighting in stairways	❑	❑
Handrails on both sides	❑	❑
Light switches at top and bottom	❑	❑
Steps even and in good shape	❑	❑
Carpet not worn and firmly fixed to the floor	❑	❑
Step edges are visible	❑	❑
No rugs at top or bottom of steps	❑	❑
No objects on the stairs	❑	❑
Non-skid contrasting tape on single step	❑	❑
Non-skid contrasting tape on non-carpeted stairs	❑	❑
Block off stairs on top	❑	❑

(Continued on the next page)

Is Your Care-Receiver's Home Safe? *(Continued)*

BATHROOM	YES	NO
Nightlight	❑	❑
Stick-on strips on floor of tub and shower	❑	❑
No throw rugs	❑	❑
Grab bars around the tub, shower and toilet	❑	❑
Shower seat	❑	❑
Bathroom commodities including plastic cup within reach	❑	❑
High-rise toilet seats	❑	❑
Hand-held showerhead	❑	❑
KITCHEN		
Appliances in perfect working order	❑	❑
Faucets easy to use	❑	❑
Adequate workspace	❑	❑
Reachable dishes, silverware and glasses	❑	❑
No wax on floors	❑	❑
Spills wiped up immediately	❑	❑
Marked stove controls	❑	❑
Regularly used items within easy reach	❑	❑
Cabinets easy to open and reach	❑	❑
Small appliances on the counter top	❑	❑
Fire extinguisher by the stove	❑	❑
Sharp objects safely stored	❑	❑
No spoiled foods in the refrigerator	❑	❑
BEDROOM		
Doorway clear	❑	❑
Raised bed if too low	❑	❑
Clothes in closet and drawers reachable	❑	❑
Clear and lit path to the bathroom	❑	❑
Floor clear of clutter	❑	❑
Light and phone by the bed	❑	❑
Bed easy to get in and out of	❑	❑
Bed rail if needed	❑	❑
Nightlight	❑	❑
LIVING ROOM		
Furniture rearranged for easy, open walking path	❑	❑
Rugs and runners removed	❑	❑
Raised seat heights if necessary	❑	❑
Bright lighting	❑	❑
Doorways clear	❑	❑
Uncluttered walkways	❑	❑
Television remote in designated spot by care-receiver's chair	❑	❑
Cords safe and away from walkways	❑	❑
Light switches marked and easy to use	❑	❑

Assistive Devices

Assistive devices can make life safer and easier for both the caregiver and care-receiver. Ask your care-receiver's medical team which items to rent or purchase, and where. They also may be able to direct you to an organization that loans these items, cost-free.

EATING

- **Adapted Feeding Utensils** – *Come in various sizes and shapes to assist with decreased hand mobility - straws, large handled utensils, cups with suction cup bottoms.*
- **Feeding Devices** – *Including a plate guard which attaches to a plate to allow one to scoop food onto eating utensils.*

DRESSING

- **Reacher** – *Assists in putting on or taking off clothing, grabbing socks or shoes.*
- **Leg Lifter** – *Assists in lifting a leg into a tub or onto a bed.*
- **Sock Aids** – *Assists in putting on socks or stockings.*
- **Shoe Aids** – *Allows one to wear slip-on shoes or use elastic shoe laces, safely and easily.*
- **Long handled shoehorn** – *Very helpful.*

BATHROOM

- **Toilet Safety Frame** – *Helps one to get on and off the toilet, especially if a solid object to hold onto is unavailable.*
- **Long Handled Sponge** – *Helps to easily reach legs, feet and back.*
- **Elevated Toilet Seat** – *Makes getting on and off safer and easier. Also available with arms.*
- **3-in-1 Commode** – *A versatile chair which can be used as a toilet riser, shower seat or as a toilet next to the bed.*
- **Bath and Shower Seats** – *A chair, with adjustable height, that can be used in the shower or tub.*
- **Tub Transfer Bench** – *Can be used when it is too difficult to step over the side of the tub.*
- **Hand-Held Shower** – *Allows the user to direct water or bathe while sitting on a tub seat.*
- **Grab Bars** – *Wall mounted grab bars, necessary to maximize safety. These MUST be anchored into wall studs.*

Is Your Care-Receiver Safe Living Alone?

This is the question a caregiver dreads. It signals a significant change in circumstances and requires a significant response. Both caregiver and care-receiver may struggle with the reality of the future as they assess needs and resources, and consider available options.

How do you know if it's time to make a change? In most cases the care-receiver's decline is gradual. First one will notice that the care-receiver needs help with a task that used to be done independently. Then he or she will need an increasing level of help. What are the markers that tell when a line has been crossed and it is no longer safe for a care-receiver to live alone? To get some indication, mark the questions below Yes or No.

YES	NO	**Regarding personal care and safety, does your care-receiver . . .**
_____	_____	remember to take medications as prescribed?
_____	_____	prepare healthy meals?
_____	_____	remember to eat?
_____	_____	remember to eat healthy?
_____	_____	feed him or herself without difficulty?
_____	_____	get dressed in appropriate clothing, get undressed without help?
_____	_____	change clothing regularly?
_____	_____	perform personal hygiene and grooming tasks daily?
_____	_____	bathe or brush teeth regularly? Shave regularly?
_____	_____	manage bowel and bladder functions?
_____	_____	move safely from bed to wheelchair, onto or off of toilet, etc.?
_____	_____	get out of a chair or bed without too much difficulty?
_____	_____	walk (can use assistive device like a cane or walker)?
_____	_____	if using a wheelchair, move from bed to wheelchair, and on and off toilet?
_____	_____	get in and out of a shower safely?
_____	_____	keep his or her balance, avoid falls?
_____	_____	keep pathways clear of items or furniture?
_____	_____	drive or arrange for transportation?
		Regarding conditions in the home, does your care-receiver . . .
_____	_____	pay bills on time?
_____	_____	keep checkbook balanced?
_____	_____	keep the house reasonably clean?
_____	_____	remember to do the laundry?
_____	_____	take out the trash?
_____	_____	use perishable food before it spoils?
_____	_____	shop for groceries or clothing?
_____	_____	use the telephone?
_____	_____	check and respond to voicemail or e-mail messages?

(Continued on the next page)

Is Your Care-Receiver Safe Living Alone? *(Continued)*

Do not over-react if you've checked No on several items on the prior page. Many of them are tasks that others can help with, allowing the person to continue living in their home.

For example, you can . . .

- Enlist family members or close friends to help with housecleaning, bill paying, grocery shopping, etc.
- Employ a housekeeper and/or a household helper to run errands, buy groceries, etc.
- Sign up for a home meal-service, use senior transportation services, and other community services that are available.

However, if you checked NO on the previous page to any of the points listed below, your care-receiver may no longer be safe living alone.

YES	NO	
___	✓	remember to take medications as prescribed
___	✓	perform personal hygiene and grooming tasks daily
___	✓	get dressed in appropriate clothing; get undressed without help
___	✓	feed him or herself without difficulty
___	✓	walk (can use assistive device like a cane or walker)?
___	✓	if using a wheelchair, move from bed to wheelchair, and on and off toilet
___	✓	manage bowel and bladder functions
___	✓	keep his or her balance, avoid falls?

In that case, it may be time for family members to take action to ensure his or her health and safety.

Steps you can take:

- Get an outside assessment of situation
- Have a family or good friend in the home at all times
- Move the person in with an adult family member or close friend
- Research area skilled-care or long-term care facilities
- Assess care-receiver's resources
- Assess family's resources
- Assess community's resources

Will Your Care-Receiver Accept Outside Help?

There may come a time when you realize the help you are getting from family members, neighbors, friends and/or your community just isn't enough. You may need a healthcare provider to come to your care-receiver's home two or more times a week to help that person bathe, dress and prepare for the day.

Care-receivers often become upset when outside help is even suggested. They may not want to listen to expressed concerns, insisting there is no problem. They want everything to remain the same. Avoid approaching the subject with a "this is the way it's going to be" attitude. Even as their choices become more and more limited, care-receivers would like to feel that they continue to have some control over their lives.

If your first attempt to approach this issue was met with anger, denial, or resistance, don't get discouraged. Accepting the need for change takes time, because it requires the care-receiver to face unpleasant or frightening facts about their present situation and the future.

They feel challenged in many ways. Beliefs they have always cherished, about how life is supposed to be, are being tested by the reality of what they are facing. Their pride is under attack, and their faith may be challenged. For those with progressive or terminal illnesses, having a healthcare professional tend to their personal needs is perhaps the most concrete indication that they are closer to the end of life.

Understanding what is behind your caregiver's resistance will help you to be patient as you go through the process of reaching an agreement and it is a process. It involves more than one conversation, some involving other family members or people who the care-receiver respects and trusts.

The following steps will help you to continue on your caregiver journey with compassion and a keen understanding of your care-receiver: There are strategies for presenting the facts in such a way that he or she will hopefully come to accept the reality of the situation. Remember that no conversation goes in a straight line from A to B to C, etc. as outlined. Bring up what seems appropriate at a given moment and, hopefully over time, you can create an environment in which your care-receiver feels safe and able to accept change.

If your care-receiver has a history of abusive behavior or shows aggressiveness related to Alzheimer's Disease or dementia, you may need the help of a professional.

(Continued on the next page)

Will Your Care-Receiver Accept Outside Help? *(Continued)*

A. Identify the thoughts, beliefs and fears that underlie the care-receiver's behavior.

This may be accomplished by brief conversations in quiet, non-stressful moments. You can ask a question while preparing a meal or helping the person get dressed. Turn a conversation about the past into an exploration of the care-receiver's beliefs. Over time, the answers you get will help you understand his/her point of view.

It is important to ask questions in the spirit of genuine interest. Your care-receiver may resist if it feels to him or her like you are probing for information.

Some underlying issues of care-receivers:
Care-receivers may believe that family members are supposed to provide care because that's what older generations did. They may think, *"If you love me, you'll care for me no matter what."* They may resist utilizing the services of public assistance programs, because *"People who are like me don't do that."*

They may have a fear of:

1) losing control of their own life and destiny
2) the presence of strangers in the home
3) the financial consequences of getting the needed help and
4) acknowledging that their situation has progressed to that level.

Finally, their need for personal privacy concerning physical functions may cause care-receivers to resist allowing a stranger to perform personal-care tasks.

B. Assess the care-receiver's physical and emotional state of mind before bringing up the topic.
Choose a time when your care-receiver is aware, alert and in a receptive mood. Resist the urge to talk about sensitive things when your care-receiver is hungry, tired, in pain or watching a favorite television show.

C. Allow your care-receiver to express his/her emotions.

- If any of the above statements are true for your care-receiver, getting outside help strikes at the heart of who the care-receiver believes him- or herself to be. Allow the care-receiver to express his/her feelings. Ask questions that encourage sharing.
- The way you approach the topic affects the way the conversation develops. Instead of saying, *"We have a problem,"* ask how things are going.
- Ask if there is something he or she would like changed. Accept the care-receiver's answers. Rather than arguing, step into his or her world.
- Ask how he or she believes the problem could be addressed. Even if you do not agree, listen to the ideas expressed. It is important the care-receiver feels heard.
- Avoid statements such as, *"That's not true."* For the care-receiver, *it is true.* Just talking about fears can help the care-receiver work through them and perhaps come to a different point of view.

D. Validate your care-receiver's viewpoint while offering your own.

When you are talking with your care-receiver, avoid saying, *"I get what you're saying, but…"* The word *"but"* creates an either/or situation. Regardless of what words actually follow *"but,"* the unspoken message of the sentence is, *"You're wrong."* That blocks the possibility of a useful exchange.

(Continued on the next page)

Will Your Care-Receiver Accept Outside Help? *(Continued)*

D. Validate your care-receiver's viewpoint while offering your own *(Continued)*

One simple change - replacing but with and - allows you to add a different dimension to the conversation. "I get what you're saying, and…" Your statement is no longer either/or. It gives space for both viewpoints to be valid. It helps the care-receiver feel valued and acknowledged and creates an opening for discussion. If your exchange gets too heated or emotional, take a break and let things cool down before continuing.

E. Ask your care-receiver for suggestions and ideas.

Even if there are few or no choices, your care-receiver needs to feel that he or she has some say in what is happening. If you've done steps A and B, ask your care-receiver for ideas and solutions. Then listen to what he or she has to say. You may be surprised at the response.

F. Explain the necessity of outside help.

A reluctant care-receiver needs to understand that bringing outside help into the home is necessary for both the caregiver and care-receiver. Explain the benefits and necessity in a kind but honest, factual, direct way.

G. Know the facts and figures.

Collect information about local agencies, the services they provide, and the cost of a home healthcare aide. Ask the care-receiver's doctor and others in the community for recommendations. If you are in contact with a support group related to your care-receiver's illness, ask members what agencies or individuals they have engaged with good results.

H. Suggest a trial phase.

Often people will do something they do not particularly want to do, if they know that it will be temporary. Ask your care-receiver if he or she is willing to give outside help a try. Let him or her have a say in which professional caregiver you will engage and the length of time for the trial phase. Hopefully, the care-receiver will see that his or her concerns and fears can be addressed in a meaningful conversation with the professional.

I. Research skilled nursing facilities and/or hospice providers before the need arises.

Nursing facility care can become necessary when the condition of the care-receiver is such that the required level of support can no longer be provided in the home. When looking for a skilled nursing facility, it is a challenge to find one that provides the level of service desired at a cost the care-receiver's insurance and funds can cover.

Hospice agencies provide a team of trained professionals to care for individuals whose "life-limiting" illness no longer responds to treatments focusing on cure. The care can be delivered at home or at the care-receiver's nursing facility. The goal is to improve the quality of life for the care-receiver by offering pain management, comfort and dignity for days, months or longer. Hospice staff also supports the family emotionally and spiritually.

J. Call on others for help.

Call a family meeting to explain the situation to family and friends so they can support your efforts. If you have taken many of the steps above and your care-receiver still resists accepting outside care, consider asking a trusted member of the medical community or clergy to speak with him or her, explaining the necessity of doing things differently for the good of all involved.

Record-Keeping

CHAPTER 7

"The biggest mistake regarding record-keeping is not writing things down or not remembering where you wrote it down."

~ David Mellem

THIS RECORD-KEEPING CHAPTER HAS THE SOLUTION! The caregiver can reproduce the tracking pages below and place them in a colorful, easy-to-find, 3-ring notebook. It is suggested that the notebook be kept in the same spot at home and taken along to all doctor appointments, hospital and emergency room visits.

The tracking pages:

1. *Caregiver's Log*
2. *Substitute Caregiver's Information*
3. *Care-Receiver Expenses Paid with Caregiver's Funds*
4. *Care-Receiver Expenses Paid with Care-Receiver's Funds*
5. *Health Care Conversation Log*
6. *Medications for* _______________
7. *Surgery and Hospitalizations for* _______________

Record-Keeping

It is important for you as a caregiver to monitor and document what is occurring over the months, and perhaps years, of caring for someone. It is for your personal benefit and for your legal protection.

Benefits of keeping the various records and logs:

- Gives you confidence and peace of mind that you are doing a good job.
- Documents that you are doing what needs to be done.
- Substantiates your assessment of the care-receiver's status and explains your choices.
- Contains data that is important when dealing with doctors and family members.
- Allows you to easily find important information.
- May protect you should anyone question your actions.

If you aren't already using these tracking methods, it's not too late to begin!

1. **Caregiver's Log** – *Examples of entries in a daily journaling log to keep for reference.* *(See page 145)*
   For **Use of My Caregiver's Log**, *(See page 146)*

2. **Substitute Caregiver's Information Log** – *Information and instructions for substitute caregivers.* *(See page 147–153)*

3. **Care-Receiver Expenses Paid with Caregiver's Funds** – *Keeping track of expenses paid out by the caregiver to be reimbursed by the care-receiver.* *(See page 155)*

4. **Care-Receiver Expenses Paid with Care-Receiver's Funds** – *Keeping track of expenditures paid by the care-receiver's funds.* *(See page 156)*

   For instructions for 3 and 4, see **Financial Records**, *page 154.*

5. **Health Care Conversation Log** – *An accounting of every phone call or interaction with health care personnel.* *(See page 157)*

6. **Medications for** ____________________ – *A complete record of all medications.* *(See page 158)*

7. **Surgery and Hospitalizations for** ____________________ – *A complete record for physicians.* *(See page 159)*

Photocopy the forms from this book, or print them from the optional e-book, and place them in a three-ring notebook.

Use of Caregiver's Log

Keeping a log is of major importance. Purchase a three-ring notebook, photocopy several copies of the page *Caregiver's Log*, and place them in the notebook for daily use. You can also use a spiral notebook or a one-page-a-day calendar. Place your *Substitute Caregiver's Information* in the beginning of your notebook. Add this page to guide you as to how to use your log. Begin writing in it as soon as possible. By noting your observations, the condition of the care-receiver and significant events such as falls, choking, or disorientation, you are creating a document that substantiates your experience with the care-receiver.

The *Caregiver's Log* can also reveal a pattern of positive changes or the worsening of a symptom. It can help you identify the issues to be addressed at a doctor's visit. It will give concrete examples of something no one else may have noticed. It can be invaluable in explaining the care-receiver's condition to family members who, for whatever reason, do not see the care-receiver often, and may not have a true understanding of what is actually happening.

You might be saying, *"One more thing for me to do? You've got to be kidding!"*

Remember, this is for *your* benefit, and for medical and legal protection. Make it a habit to write entries often, or write notes in it when you can snatch a moment or two during the day.

Your *Caregiver's Log* will include:

1. **Documentation of significant events such as a fall, choking, failure to eat or drink, trip to emergency.**
   Document with photo and text if care-receiver falls or otherwise injures himself or herself.
   Do the same if you receive an injury while caregiving.
2. **Results of a doctor, nurse, therapist and / or home health visits, especially if there are changes in your care-receiver's routine or medication.**
3. **Changes you have noticed in care-receiver's physical, mental and/or emotional state.**
   Care-receiver complains of pain more often since taking the new medication.
   Care-receiver is having more difficulty understanding me
   Care-receiver was not able to button shirt today
   Care-receiver is sleeping more
4. **What your care-receiver said about important issues. For example,**
   Care-receiver talked about fears
   Care-receiver expressed desires about funeral arrangements
   Care-receiver wants to see family members more often
5. **List of people who called you or your care-receiver, visited, or helped out in any way.**
   Care-receiver's nephew took him for a drive today.
6. **If it has been a quiet day with nothing significant to report, that is what you write down, or you might note if something went well that day.**
   *I discovered care-receiver likes it when I*_____________________________
   Care-receiver enjoys ____ *TV program*

On the following page is the Caregiver's Log template to give you an idea of what to write. You can use it as is or write on a blank page whatever you wish, still including the information on the template, when applicable.

Caregiver's Log

Date ______________________________

Significant events that happened today *(falls, choking)*: ______________________________

____

____

____

____

Results of a doctor, nurse and/or home health visit: ______________________________

____

____

____

I noticed the following changes in my care-receiver today: ______________________________

____

____

____

Today, my care-receiver said or indicated: ______________________________

____

____

____

People who called, came over or helped today: ______________________________

____

____

____

This went well today: ______________________________

____

____

____

Substitute Caregiver's Information *(Page 1)*

What you need to know when caring for ______________________________
(NAME OF THE CARE-RECEIVER)

Care-receiver prefers to be called ______________________________

Primary Caregiver Name ______________________________

Telephone Number: ____________________ Secondary Number ____________________

Travel schedule, if applicable. *(Attach)*

Emergency Information – ***person to call after you call 911 and me.***

1. **Name** ____________________ **Relationship** ____________________

   Home Phone__________ Work Phone__________ Cell Phone__________

2. **Name** ____________________ **Relationship** ____________________

   Home Phone__________ Work Phone__________ Cell Phone__________

3. **Name** ____________________ **Relationship** ____________________

   Home Phone__________ Work Phone__________ Cell Phone__________

Physicians:

Doctor ____________________ Specialty ______________ Phone Number:__________

Doctor ____________________ Specialty ______________ Phone Number:__________

Doctor ____________________ Specialty ______________ Phone Number:__________

Medications *(Attach "Medications for ____________________" chart, page 158)*

List medications to be avoided on doctor's orders.

Nearest Urgent Care	Address	Phone
Hospital of Choice	**Address**	**Phone**

Important Information: current medical condition, allergies, medical equipment (include name or provider, service and after-hour telephone numbers).

Substitute Caregiver's Information *(Page 2)*

____ **needs help with (circle all that apply)**

(NAME OF THE CARE-RECEIVER)

Bathing   Grooming   Dressing   Toileting   Eating   Walking

Getting in chair / Getting out of chair   Getting in bed / Getting out of bed

Other ____

Specific medical needs____

____

____

Specific information for items circled above:

____

____

____

____

____

Other Potential Issues: (Ex: Hearing or sight impaired, how to get up after falling, feels cold in the evening.)

Issue ____

Solution ____

Issue ____

Solution ____

Issue ____

Solution ____

Issue ____

Solution ____

Issue ____

Solution ____

Substitute Caregiver's Information *(Page 3)*

Daily Morning Routine

Wakes up at ________________ Gets out of bed at ________________

Routine for getting ready for the day________________

____

____

____

____

____

Eats breakfast at ________________

Preferred breakfast foods ________________

____

____

____

Morning medical routines ________________

____

____

____

____

Scheduled therapy ________________

____

____

____

After breakfast ________________

____

____

Has snack at ________________ Snack foods ________________

____

Takes nap at ________________

Morning activities ________________

____

Substitute Caregiver's Information *(Page 4)*

Noon and Afternoon Routine

Eats lunch at____________ Preferred lunch foods ______________________________

____

____

____

Has a snack at ________________Snack foods ____________________________

____

Takes a nap at ____

Afternoon activities ____

____

____

____

____

Evening Routine

Eats dinner at ____

Preferred dinner foods ____

____

____

Evening activities ____

____

____

____

Has a snack at ____

Goes to bed at ____

Bedtime routine ____

____

____

____

____

____

____

Substitute Caregiver's Information *(Page 5)*

Food Items' Locations ______________________________

____

____

Prescription and Over-the-Counter Meds' Locations ______________________________

____

____

Clothing Locations ______________________________

____

____

Household Information

Keys Location ______________________________

____

Mail Delivery ______________________________

Trash Pick-Up ______________________________

Recycle Pick-Up ______________________________

Information on appliances and car ______________________________

____

____

Neighbors ______________________________

____

____

Feeding and Care of Pets ______________________________

____

____

Substitute Caregiver's Information *(Page 6)*

Other Important information:

1. Schedule of all appointments (you may want to attach copy of your calendar).

____

____

2. The care-receiver likes to be called _______________
3. The care-receiver likes to talk about _______________

____

____

4. The care-receiver's interests during healthier times _______________

____

____

6. Avoid talking about _______________

____

____

7. TV or radio programs routinely watched (program name, stations or channel, day and times)

____

____

8. Preferred things to read (or be read to) _______________

____

____

9. Games to play _______________

____

____

10. Other enjoyable activities (puzzles, going for a walk, sitting outside, listening to or singing music)

____

____

____

Substitute Caregiver's Information *(Page 7)*

11. Care-receiver prefers to wear ______________________________

12. What to do when CR gets upset ______________________________

13. Other helpful information *(He does not like to be touched during a conversation. She carries her teddy bear with her where ever she goes.)*

Financial Records

You may not have thought about this important part of caregiving, but consider the following scenarios.

Mary is the caregiver for her mother who lives in the same town. She runs errands, does the grocery shopping, takes her to doctor appointments and drives wherever she wants to go. Her mother does not expect Mary to pay her bills or the gas in her car, so she writes checks to reimburse her.

Jack is a family caregiver who lives with and takes care of his parents. He also runs errands, shops, etc. and writes checks on his own account to pay their bills. Jack has so much to do and does not take the time to keep his personal finances separate from his parent's finances. Sometimes he uses their petty cash to get something he wants and sometimes he pays for something they want out of his own pocket. They settle up, but Jack often does not record it.

This way of handling expenses works just fine until another family member starts asking questions about the care-receiver's finances. Soon, other relatives are asking Mary and Jack to justify their use of the care-receiver's money. Unfortunately neither can produce complete records or receipts.

Both caregivers in these scenarios could conceivably end up feeling accused, maligned and unappreciated by family members who are content to let them carry the load of daily caregiving.

Good Record Keeping Protects Both the Caregiver and the Care-receiver

It cannot be said often enough: Keep records! Keep receipts! Keep your personal finances scrupulously separate from your care-receiver's finances. You will then be able to prove what the care-receiver's money was spent on and why.

- Keep separate receipts for items purchased for the care-receiver, using the care-receiver's funds
- If you use your funds, keep a list with receipts, a total of the amount and the check number you use from your care-receiver's account to reimburse yourself.
- Organize the receipts by month in folders, envelopes or an index file box.
- When you buy an item or pay a bill, using your care-receiver's check or cash, be sure he or she understands and agrees to the expenditure. Write the reason for the expense on the check.
- Do the same when you make a purchase from your own funds for which you will be reimbursed.
- Do the same for trips you make for your care-receiver, in your car, using your gas.
- If you are in charge of your care-receiver's checking and/or savings accounts, keep them balanced.
- Go over bank statements each month with your care-receiver, if he or she is able to understand financial matters.
- Let concerned family members know they can review books at any time.
- Consider using a specific credit card for all care-receiver's needs. The monthly statements will be a backup in case you misplace receipts for an expenditure.
- Keep track of conversations that involve caregiver and care-receiver expenses.

See *Care-Receiver Expenses*, Pages 155 and 156.
See *Health-Care Conversation Log*, Page 157.

Care-Receiver Expenses Paid with Caregiver's Funds

Date	What?	Who was Paid?	Amount	Date Reimbursed	Cash, Check or Credit Card	Receipt
Example: 1/12/2012	*Mom's blood pressure medication*	*XYZ Pharmacy*	*$32.17*	*2/1/2012*	*I charged it on my Visa*	✓

Care-Receiver Expenses Paid with <u>Care-Receiver</u>'s Funds

Date	What?	Who was Paid?	Amount	Date Reimbursed	Cash, Check or Credit Card	Receipt
Example: 2/7/2012	*Mom's health insurance*	*ABC Company*	*$328.00*	*3/1/2012*	*Monthly payment – Mom's check # 1234*	✓

Health Care Conversation Log

Date	Time	Name of Insurance Company, Physician, In-Home Health-Care	Person I Spoke With	Phone and Ext., or Email	Summary of Conversation
Example 3/4/2012	*11:37 a.m.*	*Swan Homecare Agency*	*Secretary, Jane Brown*	*123-4567*	*I explained the disagreement Dad had with the healthcare aide the agency sent to us and requested that a different person come next time.*

Medications for ______________________

CARE-RECEIVER'S NAME

Medication and Mg	Starting Date	When and How	Purpose	Side Affects	Refill
Example: XYZ 250 mg tablets	*1/12/2009*	*2 tablets – 3 times a day with food*	*Stomach pains*	*Gets dizzy*	*Every 3 months by mail*

Surgery and Hospitalizations for ______________________

CARE-RECEIVER'S NAME

Surgery/Hospitalization	Date	Physician	Location	Comments
Example: Back Surgery	*1/18/1994*	*Dr. Ben Columbus*	*Mt. Sinai Hospital Cleveland, OH*	*Laminectomy on L4, L5*

Resources

CHAPTER 8

"What's right about America
is that although we have a mess of problems,
we have great capacity – intellect – and
resources – to do something about them."

~ Henry Ford II

Resource Books

A Caregiver's Survival Guide: How to Stay Healthy When Your Loved One is Sick
by Kay Marshall Strom. InterVarsity Press Books. 2000

Chicken Soup for the Caregiver's Soul: Stories to Inspire Caregivers in the Home, the Community, and the World
by Jack Canfield, Mark Victor Hansen, LeAnn Thieman, L.P.N. Chicken Soup for the Soul. 2008

Creating Moments of Joy
by Jolene Brackey. Purdue University Press. 2008

Daily Comforts for Caregivers
by Pat Samples. Fairview Press. 1999

Giving Care Taking Care: Support for the Helpers
by Sherokee Ilse. Wintergreen Press. 1996

GriefWork for Teens – Healing from Loss (for facilitators)
by Ester Leutenberg and Fran Zamore, LISW. Whole Person Associates. 2012

GriefWork – Healing from Loss (for facilitators)
by Fran Zamore, LISW and Ester Leutenberg. Whole Person Associates. 2010

Hard Choices for Loving People
by Hank Dunn. A & A Publishers. 2009

Helping Yourself Help Others: A Book for Caregivers
by Rosalynn Carter and Susan K. Golant. Three Rivers Press. 1996

Living with Stroke – A Guide for Families
by Richard C. Senelick, MD. Healthsouth Press. 2010

One Hundred Names for Love: A Memoir
by Diane Ackerman. W.W. Norton & Company. 2011

Parting: A Handbook for Spiritual Care Near the End of Life
by Jennifer Sutton Holder and John Aldredge-Clanton. ReadHowYouWant. 2012

Passages in Caregiving – Turning Chaos into Confidence
by Gail Sheehy. William Morrow. 2010

Spiritually Sensitive Caregiving: A Multi-Faith Handbook
by Janice Harris Lord, Sharon J. English, Melissa Hook and Sharifa Alkhateeb. Compassion Books, Inc. 2008

The Caregiver Book: Caring for Another, Caring for Yourself
by James E. Miller. Willowgreen Publishing. 2008

The Complete Caregiver Support Guide – A Reproducible Workbook for Groups and Individuals
by Ester Leutenberg and Carroll Morris with Kathy Khalsa, OTR/L. Whole Person Associates. 2012

The GriefWork Companion – Activities for Healing
by Fran Zamore, LISW and Ester Leutenberg. Whole Person Associates. 2010

The Last Adventure of Life – Sacred Resources for Living and Dying from a Hospice Counselor
by Maria Dancing Heart. Findhorn Press. 2008

The Selfish Pig's Guide to Caring
by Hugh Marriott. Piatkus Books. 2009

The Validation Breakthrough: Simple Techniques for Communicating with People with 'Alzheimer's-Type Dementia'
by Naomi Feil and Vicki De Klerk-Rubin. Health Professions Press. 2002

This is Not the Life I Ordered: 50 Ways to Keep Your Head Above Water When Life Keeps Dragging You Down
by Deborah Collins Stephens, Michealene Cristini Risley, Jackie Speier and Jan Yanchiro. Conari Press. 2009

To Survive Caregiving: A Daughter's Experience, A Doctor's Advice on Finding Hope, Help and Health
by Cheryl E Woodson, MD. Infinity Publishing. 2007

Disease-Related Websites

ALS - Amyotrophic Lateral Sclerosis Association	1-800-782-4747	www.alsa.org
Alzheimer's Association	1-800-272-3900	www.alz.org
American Academy for Cerebral Palsy	1-414-918-3014	www.aacpdm.org
American Association for the Blind Society	1-800-232-5463	www.afb.org
American Association of Kidney Patients	1-800-749-2257	www.aakp.org
American Cancer Society	1-800-227-2345	www.cancer.org
American Diabetes Association	1-800-342-2383	www.diabetes.org
American Heart Association	1-800-242-8721	www.heart.org
American Kidney Fund	1-800-638-8299	www.kidneyfund.org
American Lung Association	1-800-548-8252	www.lung.org
American Parkinson Disease Association	1-800-223-2732	www.apdaparkinson.org
Arthritis Foundation and Fibromyalgia	1-800-283-7800	www.arthritis.org
Asthma and Asthma Foundation of Americ	1-800-727-8462	www.aafa.org
Brain Tumor Society	1-800-770-8287	www.tbts.org
Cancer Care	1-800-813-4673	www.cancercare.org
Celiac Disease Foundation	1-818-990-2354	www.celiac.org
Epilepsy Foundation	1-800-332-1000	www.epilepsyfoundation.org
Huntington's Disease Society of America	1-800-345-4372	www.hdsa.org
Leukemia and Lymphoma Society	1-800-955-4572	www.lls.org
MAGNUM – The Migraine National Association	1-703-349-1929	www.migraines.org
Multiple Sclerosis Foundation	1-888-673-6287	www.msfacts.org
Muscular Dystrophy Association	1-800-572-1717	www.mda.org
National Association of Anorexia Nervosa & Associated Disorders	1-630-577-1330	www.anad.org
National Association of People with Aids	TTY 1-301-587-1789 1-866-846-9366	www.napwa.org
National Association of the Deaf	1-301-587-1788	www.nad.org
National Kidney Foundation	1-800-622-9010	www.kidney.org
National Multiple Sclerosis Society	1-800-344-4867	www.nationalmssociety.org
National Organization for Rare Disorders	1-800-991-6673	www.rarediseases.org
National Osteoporosis Foundation	1-800-231-4222	www.nof.org
National Parkinson's Foundation	1-800-327-4545	
National Sleep Disorder	1-703-243-1697	www.sleepfoundation.org
National Stroke Association	1-800-787-6537	www.stroke.org
Skin Cancer Foundation	1-212-725-5176	www.skincancer.org
Spina Bifida Association	1-800-621-3141	www.spinabifidaassociation.org
United Cerebral Palsy	1-800-872-5827	www.ucp.org

Other Pertinent Websites

Aging with Dignity (Five Wishes)	1-888-594-7437	www.agingwithdignity.org
American Chronic Pain Association	1-800-533-3231	www.theacpa.org
American Pain Foundation	1-888-615-7246	www.painfoundation.org
Caregivers: Elder Care Resources and Support	Online only	www.caregivers.com
Caregiving.com	1-773-343-6341	www.caregiving.com
Centers for Disease Control and Preventions	1-800-232-4636	www.cdc.gov
Compassion Books (Caregiving, hospice, and grief resources)	1-800-970-4220	www.compassionbooks.com
Eldercare Locator	1-800-677-1116	www.eldercare.gov
Family Caregiver Alliance	1-800-445-8106	www.caregiver.org
Health Journeys / Belleruth Naperstek (Resources for Mind, Body and Spirit)	1-800-800-8661	Healthjourneys.com
Medicare	1-800-medicare	www.medicare.gov
Medicare Rights Center	1-800-333-4114	www.medicarerights.org
National Alliance for Caregiving	1-301-718-8444	www.caregiving.org
National Family Caregiver Association	1-800-896-3650	www.thefamilycaregiver.org
National Hospice and Palliative Care Organization	1-800-658-8898	www.nhpco.org
National Institute of Mental Healt	1-866-615-6464	www.nimh.nih.gov
People Living with Cancer	1-888-651-3038	www.plwc.org
Skin Cancer Foundation	1-212-725-5176	www.skincancer.org
Today's Caregiver	1-800-829-2734	www.caregiver.com
Veterans Administration	1-800-827-1000	www.va.gov/health/HealthWellness.asp
Whole Person Associates (Stress and Wellness Publishers)	1-800-247-6789	www.wholeperson.com

Whole Person Associates is the leading publisher of training resources for professionals who empower people to create and maintain healthy lifestyles. Our creative resources will help you work effectively with your clients in the areas of stress management, wellness promotion, mental health and life skills.

Please visit us at our web site: **www.WholePerson.com**. You can check out our entire line of products, place an order, request our print catalog, and sign up for our monthly special notifications.

Whole Person Associates
Books@WholePerson.com